THE WORK OF THE DEACON

AND DEACONESS

THE WORK OF THE

DEACON

AND DEACONESS

HAROLD NICHOLS

THE JUDSON PRESS • VALLEY FORGE

Standard Book No. 8170-0328-2
Library of Congress Catalog Card No. 64-15799

Sixth Printing, 1970

Printed in the United States of America

PREFACE

THIS BOOK HAS BEEN WRITTEN in the great expectation that it will help to awaken in the minds and hearts of dedicated men, women, and young people a desire to serve God and their fellow men in the high calling of the deaconship. Many concepts and methods are offered herein to suggest self-discipline, self-improvement, and a high standard of service. The reader will bear in mind that this book does not pretend to have official status; every statement must therefore be considered as suggestive.

The manuscript was developed to meet the needs of the Philadelphia Baptist Association, under whose auspices the author conducted a series of leadership training conferences for deacons. The comments and suggestions of those who participated in these conferences have helped to shape the present version.

Assuredly, the diaconate must become more effective in the life of the individual, the church, and the community. Not all the things that can be done by deacons and deaconesses are recorded in this brief volume. Notwithstanding, any methods being used successfully, whether or not they are mentioned in this book, should be continued. Even as Jesus grew in wisdom and in stature, and in favor with God and man (cf. Luke 2:52), so must the Christian who would truly follow in the master's steps. Not any one of us will become perfect in this life, but incessantly we can strive to attain the goal of perfection.

An attempt has been made to stir the imaginations of upward-looking servants of God as they take the prosaic ideas contained in this book and convert them into acts of commitment and service. It may be observed that, while the church increases in numbers and prospers materially, the work of the Holy Spirit in the life of the church has been stifled by self-satisfaction, exclusiveness, irresponsibility, and ever-lessening awareness of sin.

The deacons, as the spiritual lay leaders of the church of Christ, the body of the redeemed, are responsible to provide the energy to overcome the apathy of the church and to provide the leadership that will then be needed to guide the resulting momentum.

To acknowledge and thank all of those people who have had a part in this effort would be a completely hopeless task because I do not know the majority of them. Even an attempt to list those who have had a direct influence and helped to mold my life and thinking would be a herculean effort and the result would be a list far too large to include here. Foremost, of course, would be my family, church school teachers, youth counselors, pastors, and more-experienced deacons. Added to these would be the host of Christian friends who have played their part and wielded their influence.

Acknowledgment should also be made that my observation of the lives and examples of many who do not profess to be Christian has made me realize the blessings of God's love, and what kind of person I could have been, except for his hand working in the lives of those who have surrounded me.

My debt would not be completely stated if it did not include the authors of the many books, articles, tracts, and other kinds of Christian literature which have also influenced my life and my convictions. And, foremost and greatest, I give acknowledgment to God though Christ as he has worked in my life through the Holy Spirit and his written word.

HAROLD NICHOLS

Philadelphia, Pa.
April, 1964

CONTENTS

1

ORIGIN OF THE DEACON

AT THE REQUEST OF THE APOSTLES, the early church selected "seven men of good repute, full of the Spirit and of wisdom, whom we may appoint to this duty" (Acts 6:3). The duty? It was to serve the disciples' daily needs. In many other places throughout the New Testament there are references to various kinds of service to be performed. Paul, moreover, carefully distinguishes between bishops (pastors) and deacons, a fact which indicates that deacons were in a different category and performed a different kind of service from bishops (cf. Phil. 1:1; 1 Tim. 3:1-12).

It must be pointed out that the seven men chosen for the special tasks of caring for the widows and serving tables were not specifically called deacons in Acts 6. First, and foremost, they were called to perform a service. When the term "deacon" is used subsequently in the New Testament, it is generally assumed that it refers to men who were performing service similar to that which was assigned to the original seven who were selected. This assumption seems logical when it is understood that the Greek word from which "deacon" is derived usually describes the work of a

1

servant. Whether or not there was a difference between the tasks described in the Book of Acts and that which might be called the office of deacon in the church seems today to be inconsequential. The fact is that these people performed the work of serving; therefore they may be called deacons, or those who serve.

With the passing of time and the growth of the Christian church came more specific definitions of the responsibilities of church officers. By the time of Ignatius (about A.D. 100) there were three orders of clerics: bishop (minister), presbyter, and deacon, of whom the deacon was the lowest in rank. Not only this early concept, but subsequent growth of the idea of the cleric as set aside from the laity, has caused great divisions between Christian bodies.

Today the concept and duties of the deacon vary considerably from communion to communion. The Roman Catholic deacon is the assistant at the altar and is a member of the priesthood. The deacon in the Church of England is a member of the priesthood; he is given such ritualistic tasks as reading the gospel and assisting the priest, but he cannot consecrate the sacramental elements or pronounce absolution. The deacon in the congregational type of church is a layman who is chosen by the church. It is with the last of these types that this book is concerned.

2

REQUISITES AND QUALIFICATIONS

No AMOUNT OF DEVOTION, ability, and preparation can be considered as overabundant for a person who serves as a deacon. There must be rapport with God, an aptitude for the kind of serving that the office requires, and a thorough training in the opportunities and skills of the deaconship. About the training more will be said later. This chapter will review some of the more important features of readiness for service in the office.

Two major concepts of readiness are offered: requisites and qualifications. Generally speaking, although these terms are similar, requisites may be thought of as the person's relationship with God, while qualifications may be considered to be the person's relationships with men, and with all of the circumstances of contemporary life.

REQUISITES

According to the dictionary the meaning of "requisite" is "That which is required, indispensable, or essential." In the sincere conviction of the meaning of this word and its relationship to the work of the deacon, the following is submitted as at least a partial list of the requisites of a deacon. It would be presumptuous for anyone to attempt to make a complete list of requisites which would be binding on all those who serve the church in the office of deacon, but some things are fundamental in the life of the person who would accept the call to serve in this office. This section will contemplate only his relationship with God.

1. *A convicted person.* "All have sinned and fall short of the glory of God" (Rom. 3:23). A belief in the truth of this scriptural statement and a knowledge that it applies to himself is essential to the person who would be a deacon. There are many church members who are not convinced that they are sinners, because they see sin only in the light of the big evils of the times. If a person has no recognition of sin in his own life, how can he help others to a knowledge of God and to forgiveness of their sins through the reconciling Christ?

2. *A redeemed person.* "They are justified by his grace as a gift, through the redemption which is in Christ Jesus" (Rom. 3:24). With the acknowledgment of sin in his life, the deacon must have the knowledge that he has been redeemed by God in Christ. Other passages on this subject are: "You know that you were ransomed . . . with the precious blood of Christ" (1 Pet. 1:18, 19); "For by grace you have been saved through faith; and this is not your own doing, it is the gift of God" (Eph. 2:8). To redeem means "to buy back; ransom." The fact that this redemption has occurred in his own life makes it possible for the deacon to help others to this same saving knowledge.

3. *Baptized by immersion.* Although baptism by immersion is not a test as to whether a person is a Christian, it remains true that many churches which have deacons practice baptism by this mode. In churches where baptism by immersion is required for membership, it goes without saying that any deacon who serves therein will have observed this standard. Furthermore, even in an open membership church or a church of more than one kind of membership basis, the author of this book strongly feels that a deacon's convictions should demand that he set an example by his own baptism by immersion.

4. *Conversant with the Holy Bible.* The deacon should have more than a casual knowledge of God's Word. In it is recorded the history of the Hebrew people and of God revealing himself in their lives as individuals and as a nation. Words of wisdom and counsel are there for guidance. The revelation of God through Christ is there to bring the individual back after the separation caused by sin. The story of the early church and the lives of the early Christians is recorded for his encouragement, guidance, instruction, and inspiration. In the deacon's busy life, the reading of Scripture must not be neglected nor given only such time as he may conveniently find available. The life and work of the deacon demand that casual readings be replaced by planned study; that time be given to searching the Scriptures for their meaning to him and his life.

5. *A person with a prayer life.* A deacon must practice unceasing prayer if he is to be able to find the fullness of the Christian life for himself, and, more, if he is to be a leader among the people. Prayer is the avenue for man to com-

municate with God and God with man. Thought will not open the way; neither will works, as important as these are in the kingdom work. But prayer will open the way for God to give direction to both thought and action, so that they can be made to conform to his will and be fruitful for him. In prayer the deacon can discover for himself the glory of God, offer his praise and thanksgiving, make intercession for others and their needs, and make petitions for himself and his needs. Through his own prayer life he can then be an example in the corporate prayer life as well as being able to assist other persons to a more meaningful relationship with God through prayer.

6. *A person who worships.* Worship experiences are an essential part of the deacon's life. In his personal relationship with God and as a leader in his home, worship plays an important role. Here is the deacon's opportunity to help each member of his family to grow in the personal worship life. Public worship provides the deacon with the privilege of participation in a corporate adventure with God; of communion with him in the most favorable surroundings and with those who, like him, seek a worship experience.

The deacon has the opportunity to show his need for worship experiences by his faithful attendance at the Sunday and midweek worship services and at the business meetings of the church. He thus sets the example for the other members of the church, especially those who have recently been added to the fellowship.

7. *An example.* In every facet of Christian living not heretofore mentioned, the deacon should try to live as an example of "the new person in Jesus Christ."

Acts 2 "they met every day!" [handwritten margin note]

QUALIFICATIONS

Whereas we have chosen to gather up the spiritual constitution of the deacon under the term "requisites," those essential characteristics of Christian dealings with others which a person should possess in order to be a deacon may be termed "qualifications."

What are the qualifications of a deacon? Paul gives young Timothy a list of the things which a man should possess if he is to qualify as a deacon (cf. 1 Tim. 3:8-13):

1. Serious
2. Not double tongued
3. Not addicted to much wine
4. Not greedy for gain
5. Must hold the mystery of the faith with a clear conscience
6. Be tested first; then if he proves himself blameless let him serve
7. Be married only once
8. Manage children and home well

He continues: "for those who serve well as deacons gain a good standing for themselves and also great confidence in the faith which is in Christ Jesus."

Let us look at these qualifications in the light of today's language and see their import for the present-day deacon.

SERIOUS

The deacon shall be dignified in his appearance and manner; he shall have high ideals and practice them in his contacts with others; he shall enjoy life without indulging in the kinds of frivolities which lower the character. Deacons as a class have sometimes been accused of taking their jobs too seriously. What their critics often mean is that they are too serious-looking while they are about their work, and do not show on their faces the joy which they have in their hearts. As a sign of an inward condition, a smile can be worn in serious moments and trying circumstances. For example, Jesus' ability to influence so many lives must indicate that he possessed dignity; but, on the other hand, his ability to draw great throngs, especially children, must show that he enjoyed life. The deacon should be even-tempered and not easily disturbed. He should be the exponent and example of that love which Paul explains to the church at Corinth (see 1 Cor. 13:4-7).

NOT DOUBLE-TONGUED

The deacon shall have truth in his heart and mind, speaking to all men only that which he feels and believes. He will not say to any person anything which he would not say to all people in the same way. He will not straddle the fence by saying something to one person and the opposite of that thing to another, nor will he intentionally say anything which could be misinterpreted or have a double meaning. He will avoid situations in which he would be untrue to himself.

NOT ADDICTED TO WINE

In the time of Jesus and Paul, wine was used as a substitute for water because of the scarcity and lack of purity of water. In all of recorded history there have been some who have overindulged in strong drink and the warning here is against such a practice by a deacon. If Paul were living today, in view of the fact that water is plenteous and pure, he would probably say: "not given to drinking intoxicating beverages."

NOT GREEDY

The desire for an income which will provide the physical possessions to live comfortably and offer some protection against emergencies and retirement is not wrong. Nowhere is it recorded of Jesus that he blamed those who were blessed with more money than others. However, he was very critical of those who put their possessions first. This promotes the desire to acquire something which someone else has. One realizes that the Bible throws much light on acquisitiveness when he reads such passages as those about Zaccheus, the widow's mite, the rich young man, and the parable of the rich farmer.

There are those whose economic situation requires employment in a second job if their total income is to provide adequately for their families. When a person has two jobs he may have little or no time to devote to the deaconship, and therefore careful consideration should be given as to whether he should be called upon to serve as a deacon as long as these circumstances continue.

PERSONAL FAITH

A deacon must ever be confident in matters of doctrine and personal faith. He will recognize the Bible as the source of truth, as God's Word and will for his life and for the world. Where the understanding of the Bible's teachings becomes difficult, he will then begin to exercise faith, in accordance with Jesus' teachings. When offering some last-minute instruction to his flock, Jesus said that there would be some things which would later be declared by the Spirit of truth (cf. John 16:12-15). When he met with Nicodemus he used physical examples to teach spiritual truth, and demonstrated to Nicodemus that a man must have faith to accept that which seems to be incomprehensible. Moreover, Paul and Peter warned against vacillation (cf. Eph. 6:10-17; 2 Pet. 2:1 ff.). Such faith may sometimes, though not always, be found difficult by many of the people in the church, particularly those who base all their judgments only upon scientific data or philosophical thought. The existence of such people makes it all the more imperative that the deacon be an inspiring leader in doctrine and faith.

A PROVED ONE

A deacon should seem to be "blameless" when subject to some observation. This is not a demand for the perfection which no human being can achieve, but is, nonetheless, a suggestion that there be a high level of conduct. The judgment will include the deacon's character, churchmanship, ability, and his desire to be of service. These qualifications should be demonstrated in business and society outside the church as well as in it.

MARITAL STATUS

Among the qualifications listed by Paul is: "Let the deacons be married only once" (1 Tim. 3:12). In the days in which Paul lived and wrote, there were some men who had more than one wife at the same time. Although we do not know how prevalent the practice of polygamy was among the Jews of that time, we do know that they had the habit of adopting the customs of surrounding peoples. Also, as gentiles became Christian they did not always drop the habits and customs of their pre-Christian lives. Today, this is a serious handicap to evangelism in some areas overseas where the discarding of wives by a man would not only impose the social problem of status in the tribe for these women, but also a serious economic maladjustment. A man with such an entanglement would have neither the time nor the inclination to serve God as he should. The physical aspects of his existence would predominate over the spiritual. In addition, the man would not have the consolation and help which a wife can offer.

Some people interpret Paul's words to mean that a person who has remarried cannot rightfully hold the office of deacon, because he then would have had more than one spouse. This theory should be scrutinized very closely by a church before it makes a decision to accept or eliminate a remarried person for the deaconship. Consider, for example, the individual who is living an exemplary Christian life and possessing the requisites and qualifications for becoming a deacon, whose spouse is called by God out of this life. Perhaps such a person is already a deacon. Later, he remarries. It would be hard to believe that such a remarriage would deplete his spiritual life or his ability to serve. On the contrary, the person's loss and sorrow may deepen his spiritual experience. A more difficult case to decide is that of a person who, before becoming a Christian, was such a sinner as to be di-

vorced by his mate, but who subsequently follows Christ and
becomes a new person. He has then become "A new creation; the old has passed away, behold, the new has come"
(2 Cor. 5:17). One who has been redeemed from such a sin-
ful life has much more for which to be thankful to God and
more to give in service for him. Shall such a one, who is
otherwise qualified to serve as a deacon, be denied the opportunity to serve in this capacity? Much thought needs to
be given to these few words written by Paul, lest they be
wrongly interpreted.

This statement of Paul's is interpreted by others as dis-
qualifying all single persons for the office of deacon. These
people believe that a person cannot be a deacon unless he
is married. He can. Actually, being married does not necessarily equip one to do a better job in the deaconship. While
it might provide a conversation opener, it would not necessarily be of help in rendering counsel or service. Paul, a
single man, gave a considerable amount of advice and counsel regarding family life and relationships (cf. 1 Cor. 7; Eph.
5, 6; Col. 3; 1 Tim. 2, 5).

Some say that a single person, because of a lack of practical experience, is unable to give advice in certain situations.
But such an objection applies equally to the married person
in most instances. If there is doubt that a single person can
treat a given situation, it is probably better to send two,
whether they be single or married. Some situations are best
dealt with by deaconesses, and others by a deacon and a
deaconess together. Surely, the mere acquisition of a spouse
does not suddenly enable one to be a good servant of Jesus
Christ!

EFFICIENCY AT HOME

A deacon must manage his children and his home well. Again we must note that social conditions have changed since the days of Paul. Women have a more independent way of life and a more equal footing educationally, morally, and economically, while children seek independence at a much earlier age. The control of the family by sheer male dominance no longer exists. Order in the family comes about as the result of cooperative action. Obtaining this cooperation, that the life of the family may run smoothly, proves the ability of today's deacon to manage his home.

MORE QUALIFICATIONS

Besides the eight foregoing qualifications mentioned by Paul, there are others, some of which we shall now discuss.

A deacon should be devoted to his task. There are many opportunities to serve. Most tasks are pleasant, but some are disagreeable and difficult. The manner in which the less pleasant tasks are carried out tests the deacon's devotion.

The deacon should possess wisdom above and beyond that of the average lay person. Although formal education is of extreme importance to a deacon, and the more of it he has the more able he is to fill his office, the greatest wisdom is not found in books and education. True wisdom comes from love, understanding, and concern for others. This kind of wisdom works with God to discover avenues of service. The deacon will practice Jesus' injunction to "be wise as serpents and innocent as doves" (Matt. 10:16).

The judicious use of time is so essential to being a good

deacon that it may be called a qualification. Even though a person has the other qualifications, he cannot be an efficient deacon if he is unwilling or unable to devote the time required for fulfilling the obligations of the office. Time is as much a trusteeship as money and other possessions. The honest use of time involves putting first things first. It is the choice of spending time on that which is best, not on something that is only second best.

Where the deacons have the responsibility for the finances and property of the church, it is necessary that they be good businessmen. In areas where the church operates as a corporation, some deacons might be designated to serve as trustees. Some knowledge of law and business is mandatory in such situations.

QUESTIONS FOR DISCUSSION

1. When choosing a deacon or a deaconess, would a church ever be justified in waiving any of the requisites?

2. What would be the effect of less rigid requisites and qualifications upon the church's spiritual life and outreach?

3. What influence should a person's age have upon his readiness to become a deacon?

4. If it is admitted that no individual possesses all the requisites and qualifications described in this chapter, how can a church determine which ones may be missing without jeopardizing the work of the individual or the church?

5. How is an individual deacon affected as he works on a board of deacons composed of other individuals, each having different requisites and qualifications?

3

ORGANIZATION

A WISE MAN ONCE WROTE: "Where there is no vision, the people perish" (Proverbs 29:18 KJV). In a peculiar way, this thought applies to the work of the board of deacons. The deacons should be those who are nearest to the spiritual needs of the people. No church can grow unless it is led, not only by precept, but by example. The deacons should provide such leadership. It is in this spirit that they must view their labors.

The board of deacons should be organized to meet the needs of the church of which it is a part. Basic functions are the same in every church. Members and non-members alike have needs which can be satisfied only by the church. Spiritual needs of individuals are the same everywhere, regardless of the size or location of the church. Temporal needs vary, both in content and degree, depending on such factors as the size and location of the church. These differences make it impossible to establish one format which can be used in every church. The pattern of organization suggested herein may be followed precisely, but, more than likely, it would have to be tailored to the local situation.

The work of the board of deacons may be confined and restricted to a few specific tasks or it may be broad and extended into many areas related to the mission of the church. Some questions arise in respect to the work which should be considered as proper for the deacons. How does a board of deacons take care of all the tasks that may possibly challenge it? How much of the work has been delegated or relinquished to other groups, committees, or boards? How much is not being done at all? Is the board so organized as to be functioning efficiently and effectively? Are there enough deacons on the board to care for the needs of all the members and the community? The facts in this chapter would naturally lead one to ask such questions as the foregoing ones.

It is to be regretted that in many churches there are important areas of work for which the deacons should hold themselves responsible, but in which they fail. Such failure comes by indifference, inefficiency, lack of vision, or perhaps mere oversight. In churches where this has occurred, it often happens that some action which should have fallen in the province of the board of deacons is carried out by an individual, or some group other than the deacons, or by the entire church.

In order that a board of deacons may keep in mind its necessary functions, it is proposed that there be committees on ordinances, worship, watchcare, unchurched, and finances. Of course, the number of committees may vary with the size of the board of deacons, and, to some extent, the size and needs of the church. Smaller boards may combine two or more of the areas of work, and larger boards may further divide some of the areas to form more committees. In any event, these areas are all within the responsibilities of the board of deacons, and none should be overlooked.

A further suggestion may be in order regarding individual deacons. This is a day of specialists, when the Jack-of-all-trades is becoming less and less useful. The basic method for the board of deacons to obtain conservation of time and energy is the development of specialists among the deacons who will concentrate upon one, or a few related, functions. This method will permit each deacon to carry out his own functions smoothly, and become adept in handling problems and difficult situations of a special nature. The extent to which such specialization can be developed depends upon the local church.

NUMBER OF DEACONS

Some interpret the selection of the seven disciples by the church at Jerusalem as constituting the first board of deacons. There are churches which maintain exactly seven deacons, and hold that any other number is not biblical. Such a view ignores the tremendous growth of the church and the changes which have occurred since that time.

In small churches seven deacons would be too many; in many medium-sized and all large churches, a restriction to seven would seriously handicap the work: tasks would not get done and what was done would be inadequate, inefficient, and possibly ineffective.

A more logical method to determine the number of deacons in a church is to decide how many members or families a deacon could serve. It is also important to remember that a deacon should have no other major office in the church and that the greater portion of his visiting and serving must be done in the evenings. The number of deacons may then be fixed by providing a deacon for every ten families, or for every fifty members, with a minimum of three deacons.

Some churches consider every officer to be be a deacon. This makes the board of deacons very large. From this large body of deacons, specialists serve in whatever capacities the church may need. For example, business-minded members serve as trustees and are the legal custodians of the church property; educators serve in the field of Christian education; other talented ones have responsibilities as treasurers, secretaries, or any other function. This plan has much merit, for it provides that every office be filled by a person motivated by a spirit of unity which is not always to be found otherwise. This plan also reduces the number of boards and committees, and avoids duplication of effort.

Whatever the plan of organization may be, each local church should determine how many deacons are required to meet its needs. There should be enough deacons so that each one can do an effective job and serve the members of the church and the people of the community as he should. The number of deacons should be specified in a church's by-laws. An escalator clause based on the number of members or families would permit an automatic change in the number of deacons.

SELECTION OF DEACONS

There are various ways by which a church can select its deacons. Three possible methods are noted here, although some churches may discover other methods that, for themselves, meet with success.

The most common method of choosing deacons is for the church to select a nominating committee which will submit the names of nominees for church action. Before the selection of any person for any office in the church, much thought, investigation, and prayer are required, but for the office of deacon it is doubly important that this be done. In some churches the board of deacons, through its representative on the nominating committee, suggests the names of persons whose qualifications are such as to justify consideration. Nomination by a nominating committee followed by election by the church affords the opportunity to select those who are best qualified for this important post.

A second method of obtaining deacons is that of inviting nominations from the floor of a church business meeting, without previous preparation. There are hazards in this method which may prevent the church from securing the best-qualified individuals for the office. It is conceivable that names could be put before the congregation as a reward for long membership, as a token of friendship, or for some selfish motive. Moreover, when more than one person is proposed for an office in an open business meeting, the loser is usually embarrassed, and sometimes bad feelings are left.

A third method sometimes practiced gives the board of deacons the responsibility of presenting the names of nominees directly to the church for action. The advantage in this procedure is that the deacons themselves are in the best position to determine the kind of person who is needed to fulfill the duties of the office. However, this method may leave the board of deacons vulnerable to a charge of self-perpetuation. Whether such a charge were later proved valid or invalid, the result would be an unwelcome bad feeling in the church.

In making the selection of deacons, certain practical considerations should be kept in mind. It is well if a deacon has no other major office or responsibility. Because of the wide scope of deacons' responsibilities, consideration might be given to the selection of those who have specialized qualifications or skills, to perform specific tasks. The church's by-laws should clearly specify the method of selecting deacons.

TERM OF OFFICE

There are many ideas concerning the length of a deacon's term of office and the total number of consecutive years an individual may serve in the office. Some churches elect members for life, on the premise "once a deacon always a deacon." Some churches specify for deacons a limited term of office, but habitually reelect any number of times those whose terms expire. This is almost the same as the maintenance of life deacons. Many churches have discovered that a rotation of the personnel on the board is the most workable plan. This provides that, after serving one, two, or three full terms, an individual cannot be reelected to the office until a year has elapsed. If a term of office is three years and a deacon may be reelected twice, the full span of service will then be nine years. After this individual has been off the board for a full year he is again eligible for election and reelection as before.

There are several distinct disadvantages in the practice

of electing deacons to serve for life. Some deacons prove to be unworthy or incapable. In the second place, deacons do not escape the advancing years and the accompanying diminishing of mental and physical strength. Moreover, the rising age-level of all of the deacons may result in such a high average age that the outlook becomes static and the work handicapped. Another drawback in the general picture of the work of the church is that many other departments and offices are penalized by the fact that they cannot be occupied by those whose former deaconships have given them rich experiences. Finally, life deaconships restrict the number of those who can be trained in the work of the deacon.

Much can be said in favor of rotation. If a person proves to be worthy of continued service as a deacon, an occasional mandatory year of inactivity will not be serious. When a constantly changing personnel is a possibility, the unworthy ones can be eliminated without danger of injured feelings, and younger persons can be added to the board.

What, then, can be done to honor the faithful servant who has labored long and nobly in the deaconship, but who has obviously come to the age when retirement is best for himself and the church? Here is the situation in which the church may gracefully and lovingly bestow upon such an individual the title of "deacon emeritus." As such, he retains the respect and honor of the office, but does not bear its problems and responsibilities.

The length of a term and the number of consecutive terms that are permissible should be stated in the by-laws. It is suggested also that the by-laws make clear that the filling of an unexpired term does not count when reckoning the number of terms served.

INDUCTION

There are a number of ways in which deacons can be inducted into office. All of these ways serve the purpose of impressing the new deacons with the seriousness of their tasks and the appropriateness of their service.

Ordination is one way of induction. The proponents for this method go back to the biblical record of the ancient church at Jerusalem which says: "These they set before the apostles, and they prayed and laid their hands upon them" (Acts 6:6). This practice seems to be most logical in those churches which have life deacons. This interpretation follows the theory that, as ministers are called and ordained into service, so are deacons.

Installation is another type of induction. This embraces calling the deacons (or perhaps all officers) to the front of the sanctuary to engage in a brief initiatory service led by the pastor.

Recognition is a third possible manner of induction to office, in which case the names of the deacons (or perhaps all newly-elected officers) are printed in the church paper and/or read by the pastor from the pulpit.

Fourthly, the deacons may be publicly introduced into office by a consecration service, in which the deacons are called to the front of the sanctuary.

Then the pastor, deacons, and congregation all participate in a service of consecration, as all three commit themselves to serving and assisting.

No matter what type of introduction or induction to office is used, it should be conducted in a worshipful, dignified manner so as to be an inspiration to all who take part in the service or witness it.

For one reason or another, a vacancy may occur at any time. When this happens, early action is imperative, lest the work suffer and the church become ineffective. Resignation from office, removal to another church, and death are common reasons for the creation of a vacancy. But there is another, more involved, reason.

Occasionally it happens that a deacon neither dies, moves away, nor resigns, but, for some reason, fails to be useful to the church and the whole cause of Christ. He may lose interest, refuse to perform his obligations, fail to find the time, become ill, or grow too old and infirm. The first three of these are attributable to the deacon himself; the last two are beyond his control.

A deacon may show his lack of interest by failing to attend the regular meetings of the board and by continually neglecting his assignments. Some churches set a limit upon the number of consecutive absences without excuse, thus bringing to light the deacon's lack of interest. Refusal to perform obligations sometimes occurs when a deacon discovers, after he has been elected and installed, that the duties are more difficult than he expected them to be. This can easily happen if someone fails to explain to him the responsibilities of the office when he is being asked to serve. Another kind of surprise which awaits some newly elected deacons is the amount of time which must be devoted to the task, often when personal or family obligations seem to interfere. Here again is the picture of an office holder who finds that he must make choices as to how to use time, and who chooses not to use it for the accomplishment of his duties. All of these untoward situations result in decreased efficiency and the neglect of members. When the work thus suffers, some kind of immediate remedial action is needed.

The first step to take in the case of a nonperforming deacon is to have a frank talk with him. This may be done by one of the deacons, perhaps the chairman of the board or the oldest deacon. In some cases the interview may need to be the pastor's responsibility. If the first interview proves to be fruitless, several or all of the deacons should call upon him for a second interview. All of this should be conducted with the utmost of Christian understanding, kindness, courtesy, and love, and with the hope that the erstwhile defective deacon may be restored to a happy working relationship (see Gal. 6:1-6).

There will be occasions, however, when interviews do not result in the resumption of a satisfactory relationship. Even in a case like this, it should be remembered that the one who is withholding his willing service was held in such high regard that he was entrusted with the office. Whether or not some provision in the by-laws has automatically removed him from office, his acquiescence to resign should be obtained. This should be done only after every effort by persuasion, counseling, and prayer has been exhausted. Again let it be emphasized that this should be accomplished kindly and in an atmosphere of good Christian spirit.

The problem which arises when a deacon becomes ill or infirm is quite different. Here is a person who perhaps has been fulfilling an invaluable place in the life of the church for a long time, and who undoubtedly wishes that he might continue to do so. In some instances, the church can honor such a person by electing him to be deacon emeritus. This automatically creates a vacancy on the board of deacons, but continues throughout the remainder of the individual's life to speak of the esteem in which he is held.

Now let us assume that the church's by-laws have provided for the elimination of deacons who for any reason do not meets the standard of acceptable performance; and let us further assume that a vacancy exists on the board of deacons. What shall be done, and how shall it be handled? Unless the church year is nearly concluded, the vacancy should be filled promptly, so that the work of the board will not suffer.

One way of filling a vacancy is by the work of the nominating committee, which, in many churches, is on call to serve at any time during the year. When notified of the need, the nominating committee may meet and present a suitable name or names for an early special election by the church. Other methods of filling the vacancy include nomination by the deacons followed by church election, church election without benefit of previous nomination, and appointment by the deacons to serve either for the remainder of the church year or for the remainder of the unexpired term. In any case, the by-laws should clearly state what procedure is to be followed, and impose a time limit for filling the vacancy.

QUESTIONS FOR DISCUSSION

1. Is the board of deacons of our church organized in such a way as to perform the best possible task? How would you revise its organization?

2. Are there enough deacons in our church to provide for the needs of the fellowship and the community?

3. In our church, how many responsibilities which should belong to the deacons have been delegated or left to others?

4. What responsibilities of the deacons are being neglected or overlooked?

5. List and discuss the relative advantages and disadvantages of:

   (a) The usual method of utilizing deacons in the church's work.

   (b) The inclusion of all of the church's work under the board of deacons.

Divide those present into small groups (3 to 5 persons each) and have some groups consider (a) and others (b), and each group bring its findings before all.

4

ORDINANCES

WHENEVER A CHURCH SPIRE is seen, rising above surrounding buildings and pointing to the skies, the suggestion of upward movement comes into man's mind. By this suggestion, most persons are inspired to think about God. The ordinances—baptism and the Lord's Supper—like a church spire, are symbols which remind Christians of the deepest and most sacred aspects of the Christian faith. These two ordinances are generally regarded as the two observances of the church commanded by Jesus Christ. The deacons have much to do with these solemn symbols.

BAPTISM

Baptism is regarded as an outward expression of an inward belief. It is much more than a simple ceremony which must be performed just before a candidate becomes a member of a church. The candidate must be made to realize the importance of this event. The deacons can do much to make the experience enrich the spiritual life of the individual.

PHYSICAL ARRANGEMENTS

Long before any baptisms take place, the deacons should make certain that physical surroundings are attractive, convenient, and clean. No other group in the church will view the need for complete upkeep of this part of the property with as much interest. All facilities for the baptism, including the baptistry, dressing rooms, approaches, and equipment should be painted, well lighted, clean, and well ventilated.

When a baptismal service is planned, the deacons should see that the baptistry is filled and the water is at the proper temperature. If flowers are to be given to those baptized, these should be provided. Hair dryers should be in working order, or the women and girls being baptized should be advised to bring their own. The candidates should be thoroughly briefed as to what clothing and supplies to wear and bring with them. If the church provides baptismal gowns, each candidate should be assigned one that is clean, well fitting, and in good condition. All procedures surrounding entering the water, being baptized, and leaving the baptistry should be described in detail. Women should deal with the women and girl candidates. If the church has no deaconesses,[1] the board of deacons should select some capable women to do this work. During the service, members of the candidates' families or the deacons and their women appointees should assist the candidates. Privacy, to avoid embarrassment to the candidates, is to be sought. One church achieved this for the women and girls by providing hooded capes for them to wear when going to and from the baptistry.

---

[1] For a discussion of the deaconess, see Chapter 11.

It is advantageous to have all the foregoing instructions, with perhaps some biblical references to baptism, in printed form to hand to the candidates.

BRIEFING THE CANDIDATE

The candidate should be thoroughly instructed in the meaning of baptism. He should also be informed as to how the deacons' own church regards the rite. Furthermore, it would be helpful to him to know the interpretations of the meaning of baptism made by other churches. The candidate has probably been exposed to some of this in the church school, by the pastor, or by the board of deacons during a previous interview. However, shortly before going through this ritual, his mind should be refreshed in the Bible teachings and background regarding it, so that it will be all the more significant and impressive. One should remember that it was not easy for Christ to suffer separation from his father and be buried in a tomb, and that the experience of going through the baptismal waters is, in one sense, a reminder of the price he paid for the redemption of men.

THE BAPTISMAL SERVICE

The time of baptism is optional. It may be morning or evening, during the worship service or following it. When baptism is at the conclusion, the candidates and attendants can attend the first part of the service, sitting near an exit, and leave quietly during a hymn shortly before the baptism, coincidentally with the pastor's departure. The candidates should be robed or dressed and ready for baptism before they enter the sanctuary for the worship service.

If the church does not have a convenient exit, or if they so prefer, the candidates and attendants may wait outside the sanctuary (perhaps a room could be provided with an amplifier so they can hear the service). If this arrangement is not possible, some type of service might be provided for them under the direction of the deacons.

Having the baptism at the early part of the worship service provides an opportunity for the candidates and attendants to participate in the latter part of the service. The pastor can conduct the opening of the worship service from the baptistry if necessary and can make his change during the hymn or anthem. This plan also enables him to greet the congregation at the close of the service.

No effort should be spared to make this a never-to-be-forgotten occasion, a memorable, richly rewarding experience, conducted in a prayerful and Spirit-filled atmosphere. Baptism by immersion is a natural and normal way for the person to show his acceptance of Christ as his Savior before the other people of God. The rite should be carried out quite naturally and without an excessive emotional display.

THE LORD'S SUPPER

The Lord's Supper, observed by the entire congregation, is the other ordinance that was specifically mentioned by our Lord as a practice for believers. The time and frequency of the observance of communion varies considerably among Christians. No scriptural directive is given; the only known precedent is that Jesus and the twelve met at night for the Passover (Mark 14:17; John 13:30; 1 Cor. 11:23).

FREQUENCY OF OBSERVANCE

A widely practiced time for the Supper is the morning of the first Sunday of each month and on such special or seasonal occasions as Maundy Thursday, Christmas, Watchnight, or candlelight services. In addition to these, an occasional evening communion service would permit participation by some who are unable to attend morning services because of their being occupied as nurses, public servants or caring for a young child or an invalid at home. In those churches which have an expanded church school session, a class for children, or a nursery during the worship service, there are leaders or teachers who are unable to participate in the communion service. In such churches, if the staff is sufficient in number, a rotation might be worked out so that all might participate at some time. When rotation is not possible, these people might share in an observance of the Lord's Supper after the regular service has been concluded.

The custom of holding the communion service after the close of or near the end of a regular worship service stems from the practice of closed communion, before which those who are not members of the church are offered a convenient opportunity to depart. Some churches continue to observe closed communion, and in these the old custom of putting it at the conclusion persists. The break which occurs between the worship service and the communion service often allows a loss of the sense of worship and dedication which is never recovered. Such timing is likely to imply that the observance of the Lord's Supper has only a secondary importance.

A much better plan is to make worship and communion

one continuous service. This will cause a minimum of disturbance and distraction. One church has solved this by having the pastor and deacons assume their positions at the table during the singing of a hymn. When the congregation is seated, the deacons receive the fellowship offering, the pastor brings the morning message, and the elements are then served immediately. In this way there is very little disturbance. In some churches the deacons assume their positions for the entire worship service, but this practice may deprive the choir of members who are deacons.

PRACTICAL POINTERS

A number of things can be done to make this service of commemoration helpful and vital. Preparation for the Lord's Supper includes making certain that the linen is cleaned and ironed, the bowl and napkin are ready for the pastor (if he uses them), the trays and glasses are polished and clean, the elements are freshly prepared, the table arranged, the offering plates in place, and the chairs ready.

Each deacon should know exactly what he is to do and what is his part in the service so that no confusion and awkward situations arise to detract from the solemnity of the service. The author's church has fifteen deacons, of whom eight sit with the pastor and serve the elements; one leads in the reading of the covenant and two lead in prayer. The other deacons come forward with the eight but take seats in the first pew. Assignments are on a rotation basis as described on the seating chart in the Appendix. The chairman or some delegated deacon should know exactly who will be absent so any change can be made in advance.

CONDUCTING THE SERVICE

In many churches, the pastor offers the prayers during the communion service; in many others it is the deacons who do so. Without doubt, the pastor's prayers will be delivered more smoothly, but there is great value in the deacons' participation. When a deacon is to be called upon to lead in prayer, he should be so informed in advance, for some deacons cannot pray spontaneously.

In most churches the fellowship offering is received by the deacons prior to the serving of the elements. This is another act which seems like an interruption in the midst of the service. It is possible that this offering could be received with the offering which is received during the opening portion of the service. Special communion envelopes located in the pews could be used for this purpose.

The important thing to bear in mind is that the dignity, solemnity, and worshipful atmosphere should be preserved. This ordinance is a memorial service to the Lord and everything in it should honor and glorify his name.

QUESTIONS FOR DISCUSSION

1. How often should baptismal services be held?
2. What can a deacon do to enrich the spiritual life of a candidate for baptism?
3. Does the frequency of observance of the Lord's Supper affect its meaning?
4. How can the Lord's Supper be made available to every member of the church?

5

WORSHIP

THE WORSHIP OF ALMIGHTY GOD is central in the needs of the Christian. As in other areas of the life of the church member, the deacon has an opportunity to provide the most favorable conditions for meaningful worship experiences. Physical surroundings, assisting the pastor in making arrangements for regular or special services, helpful ushering, and securing the attendance of worshipers are all a part of the preparation in which the deacons, to some extent, may participate.

CARE OF SANCTUARY

Nothing short of the most strict cleanliness of the sanctuary or any other room is essential to true worship. In some churches, even the observant eyes and the remonstrances of the women cannot avail to provide cleanliness. The deacons should insist that the place of worship be immaculately clean. Sometimes, with the best of care, a last-minute dusting of pews and furniture may be necessary or desirable. All that can be said about the care of the sanctuary applies equally to any room or meeting place where worship is to take place. The deacons should view all problems regarding the property as being within the province of the board of trustees. Whenever the deacons see conditions that need attention, they should therefore tactfully make suggestions to the trustees, rather than act directly.

Sometimes the sanctuary is not kept in the best of repair and small defects appear. The people get so accustomed to the defects that they do not notice them. Gradually more and more deterioration occurs without attracting attention. The need for repair goes from bad to worse, as someone says that it doesn't look too bad, or the trustees are apathetic, or funds seem to be insufficient. The deacons have a responsibility to recognize such conditions, bring them to the attention of the trustees and members, and encourage prompt action toward correction.

The comfort of the worshipers is a prime necessity for complete participation in any worship experience. Making certain that the temperature is right and the air is fresh is a must if distraction is to be avoided. In extreme heat, air-conditioning or power fans can be provided. Hand fans are tiring and distracting, while electric fans posted around the room make a hum. Both are disturbing and are often ineffective.

The preparation for worship means that hymnals and Bibles will be evenly distributed and attendance cards and pencils will be in the holders. The appearance of drapes, flags, and other furnishings should conform to the setting.

Deacons would do well to approach the sanctuary as if they were visitors seeing it for the first time, and to be as observant and critical of its appearance as visitors would be.

FURTHER MEASURES

There are a number of other important details connected with the worship services, other than the keeping of the building, which help to promote a real experience. There may be members who are unable to hear. If a hearing aid system is not already installed, the deacons should initiate a movement to obtain one which has the number and location of receivers to meet the need. The deacons should test these devices before every worship service. Many churches require a public address system because of the size or construction of the sanctuary. Sometimes such a system is installed especially to eliminate the strain on the pastor's voice. Even if the pastor has a strong voice which does not require amplification, visiting pastors or speakers may require it. A public address system will equalize voices and permit all to hear well. A deacon should test it before each service.

Flowers add to the beauty of the sanctuary, and the deacons should make certain that they are provided, either through a flower committee selected by the church, or by the board, or by certain deacons who are responsible for the sanctuary. Flowers can be given by organizations, church school classes, or by individuals. They can be given in memory of a loved one. A schedule should be maintained so that there will be flowers at every worship service. At the close of the day, the flowers can be taken to some person who is ill or shut in. Decorating the room for special occasions could be done by the same committee or by a special group chosen for the occasion. The wearing of flowers by the ushers adds another touch of beauty. In one church one family provides these flowers for every worship service.

An important aid to worship is ushering. In some churches the deacons do all of the ushering; in some, the deacons recruit ushers from the men of the congregation at each service; in others there is a well organized ushers' group; and too often the ushering will range from semi-organized to haphazard. Regardless of who does the job, the deacons should see that it is done well, with a minimum of disturbance. The best plan is to have the ushering performed by a separate group organized under a head usher, with rules governing personal appearance, deportment, dependability, punctuality, and duties.

Music is not a direct responsibility of the deacons but they should be observant for possible ways of improving this phase of the worship experience. They can often help the choir members to eliminate unnecessary movements and all talking. Most choirs are located where they are visible to the congregation, and any violation of good deportment is distracting and disturbing.

The deacons should make certain that everything is done which the pastor needs. They should make sure that his hymnbook is in its place, as well as hymnbooks for guests or other participants; that a glass of fresh, cool water is provided; that sufficient chairs are in place; and that the lights on the pulpit and lectern are working.

Prayer before the beginning of the worship service is practiced in some churches and varies in form with the desires of the pastor. Some pastors like to have the entire board of deacons meet with them; some meet with whatever deacons are free; others like to meet with the choir for prayer. The wishes of the pastor are to be respected in this matter. If the pastor does not meet for prayer with the choir, a deacon should perform this important duty.

To summarize, it is important that the deacons responsible for worship do anything and everything to make the worship experience a time of spiritual enrichment for all. Further, it is imperative that all preparations be completed well in advance of the earliest arrivals, so that those things which are being done to provide comfort, distraction-free surroundings, and a decorous atmosphere do not themselves prove to be distracting.

MIDWEEK SERVICES

In the thinking of many, there is no more important meeting in the life of the church than the midweek prayer service. This service has been called a barometer indicating the level of the spiritual life of the church and a thermometer showing how spiritually hot or cold the members are. Jesus prayed continually for himself, for his disciples, and for all who followed him. He urged his followers to pray, giving them a pattern to follow in prayer and promises of blessing and reward in God's response. In many churches there are few who attend, and, for this reason, some churches have even discontinued the service. Of all the lay people, the deacons in particular should feel a serious concern for the health of the prayer service.

There are various techniques in use to bring about successful prayer services. Some churches use the fellowship approach by having a supper before the prayer meeting; some hold board, committee, and other group meetings before or after the prayer service; others assign the responsibility for conducting the prayer meeting to various groups. The best situation, of course, is that in which fervent prayers of the concerned are offered that God will work in all members to make them concerned. In any case, the deacons must be good examples for others in regularity of attendance and participation. The deacons can help to create a worship atmosphere as they guide others in the importance of prayer.

The deacons are responsible for the leadership of this service in the absence of the pastor. In fact, the occasional leadership of the service by the deacons would not only relieve the pastor, but would also give him the opportunity to have a unique worship experience. Moreover, such leadership gives the deacons an excellent chance to improve their ability to lead and preach.

Prayer services are attractive when they are held in unusual forms. Cottage prayer meetings provide variety, and may encourage wider participation by the members because of the informality of the surroundings. They could be held at regular intervals or scheduled at random times. Several area meetings held simultaneously have a tendency to encourage greater attendance by reducing the distance to be traveled. Many people with children or night work schedules would like to attend the prayer meeting. Perhaps a prayer meeting held at a late morning or early afternoon hour would open the way for such persons to become active in their prayer participation.

PULPIT

It is the deacons who have a responsibility to see that the pulpit is occupied at each worship service. Although the pastor will usually be in the pulpit, illness, conventions, convocations, conferences, denominational office, vacation, or some other project may temporarily leave the pulpit vacant. Then the deacons must find a substitute or approve a substitute recommended by the pastor. Occasionally an outside speaker may be invited, such as an evangelist, a missionary, a representative from the denomination, or a guest speaker for some special event in the church's life. In some communities it is the practice to have a periodic exchange of pulpits, arranged by the clergy club or ministerium, or simply by the pastors of two or more churches.

There are some arrangements to be made when a guest speaker is invited. Some things will be done by the pastor, but the deacons should make certain that everything is done for the guest to assure his comfort and to make his visit as pleasant as possible. The extent of such arrangements depends on the distance the guest has traveled, his mode of transportation, and the length of his stay. If he is coming by public conveyance, arrange where and when to meet him and take him to where he is to stay. This could be in a private home or a hotel. In the latter case, make certain that a reservation has been made in advance. If he is driving, see that he has definite directions as to where to go— to the church, the parsonage, or a private home. When he is ready to leave, take him back or give him directions as to how to return. Arrange for the guest's meals, at a hotel, the parsonage, or a private home. If he has brought his wife along, she should be included in all these phases of entertainment.

In many instances, an honorarium should be given. This

should be agreed upon by the board of deacons and pastor when the decision is made to invite the guest, and it should be given to him privately before he leaves. Most visitors will be paying the expenses of their trip from their own funds, and in all fairness should not have to wait until some later date for reimbursement.

The deacons should arrange for at least one person to take the guest on a tour of the church building, especially the sanctuary, so that he may become familiar with the surroundings and the conditions under which he will speak. If the guest is a woman, a woman from the church should either lead or accompany the tour. If the pastor is away, one or more deacons should go over the order of service with the guest. A deacon should accompany the guest on the platform and, at the very least, introduce the speaker to the congregation. Most guests, especially strangers, would prefer and appreciate having a deacon lead the entire service.

A GREETING FOR ALL

The subject of welcoming will be considered in the discussion on watchcare, but only as such a greeting relates to the members and as a means for follow-up by the deacons (see p. 48). However, the act of making all people welcome has a much broader significance. Members and nonmembers alike have come to the church by exerting effort. Some have come from happy and joyous homes, but others have come from an environment of hopelessness or tragedy. Some have been undecided as to whether to come or not. But all have come that they might share their deepest feelings with other Christian people. The kind of reception they experience before, during, and after the service will be highly charged with meaning for each one.

A church gets a reputation as a friendly church or a cold church, depending on the welcome which it gives to all. It is at this point that all deacons (not just those who are on a welcoming committee) set the example for the rest of the members. It is easy for anyone to introduce himself to one who is just arriving, ask a few friendly questions, and generally make the person feel at home.

In larger churches visitors may be lost in the congregation and may be unrecognized. Some churches use a means of identification for visitors, such as badges or ribbons, but this is rather difficult when there is more than one entrance. In very large churches, even the most efficient plan will not be completely successful. If all visitors would identify themselves as they enter, the problem would be solved, but this cannot be expected. When visitors can be identified, members will feel more free to speak to them without fear of mistaking an unknown member for a visitor.

Taking time to greet and speak to those who are members is also helpful in making a friendly church. Encouraging a happy fellowship among the members is a prime responsibility of the deacons. In smaller churches this responsibility is not difficult because the members already know each other very well. In larger churches, however, it is not easy to obtain a close relationship among all the members. More than likely, each one associates with a few of his intimate friends. The existence of such groups makes it difficult for new members to feel that they are a part of the fellowship. When members pass other members in the aisles without speaking to them, how difficult it is to get them to speak to visitors and welcome them!

CHILDREN

In these busy times, there is a temptation for deacons to be so engaged with their relationships with adults that they overlook the children. Nevertheless, Jesus had time for the little ones, and there are many references in the Bible to the dedication of children to the Lord. Among the Jews, the firstborn were consecrated, according to God's command (cf. Ex. 13:1, 13-14). Examples of this are found in Samuel's dedication and in the presentation of Jesus according to the custom of the law.

The deacons should encourage the dedication of children as early as the parents are able to bring them. In this ceremony, parents are made to feel their responsibility to God and to their child. To impress them, they are called upon to recognize that the child is a trust from God, that they must be good examples of those who are growing in Christian knowledge and faith, and that they are enjoined to provide a Christian home and environment such that, when the child becomes of proper age, he will naturally desire to become a follower of Jesus Christ. A service of dedication, moreover, is a means of drawing the entire congregation closer to God as memories are stirred and as the congregation, in some degree, assumes a responsibility for maintaining a Christian community.

Through the board of Christian education and the trustees, churches frequently set up programs and accommodations for a nursery. While this endeavor is not the responsibility of the deacons, it should, nevertheless, be of interest to them. If a nursery is not already available, the deacons should be prominent in any encouragement to organize one.

There are a number of ways in which a nursery can be set up. An example of one way is the building of a sound-proof room at the rear of the sanctuary. Here the parents can be with their children and at the same time be able to see and hear the entire church service. If one-way vision glass is used, there is nothing to distract the other worshipers. Another scheme for conducting a nursery is to locate it in another section of the church building. Under this plan the parents can attend the worship service or remain with their children. If a public address system is used in the sanctuary, a speaker can be installed in the nursery for the benefit of those who are serving there.

It will be found that there are many details which must be considered. The nursery and its equipment must be made as sanitary as possible. A nurse, preferably registered, should be in charge of the nursery.

QUESTIONS FOR DISCUSSION

1. What can the deacons do to keep every member of the church active and regular in attendance, participation, and wider service?

2. Under what circumstances should a deacon be a lay preacher? Should he serve other churches in this capacity?

3. How can the board of deacons take an interest in the care of the sanctuary without arrogating to themselves the work of the trustees?

6

WATCHCARE

WORLDWIDE AND LOCAL SITUATIONS are bringing more and more stresses to bear upon the individual. No one seems to be able to escape from the frantic tenseness of an ever faster-moving tempo. It is said that not only adults, but also children, even infants, often suffer from mental illness because of worry and insecurity. In the midst of a frenzied world, the church stands as a mentor, ready to watch over and guide each individual who comes within its influence. The pastor and the deacons, as leaders in the spiritual life of the church, are interested in each person in the church for the duration of his life. The deacons have much to do in the matter of watchcare, and each facet is important to the spiritual life and growth of the people with whom they are concerned.

ASSIGNMENT OF MEMBERS

Every member of the fellowship should be promptly assigned to a deacon who serves as liaison between the church and that member. The most popular method of assigning is by parish or area, but it can also be done by age groups, mutual interest, or business contacts. Whatever scheme is adopted, the principle to be followed is to assign each member to the deacon who can best serve him. New members should be assigned in the same manner as soon as they are received. If the church has a board of deaconesses, the assignments to them should be the same as for deacons. Or, one deaconess could easily work with two or more deacons, or the deaconesses could be available for visitation at the call of any deacon. If there is a mixed board, one of the foregoing procedures could be followed, the choice of procedure to depend on the local situation. When the church has no deaconesses, the board of deacons could select qualified women of the church to serve.

Assignments should be changed after one or two years to permit each deacon to become acquainted with more members than otherwise would be possible.

To those who are new converts it should be stressed that the acceptance of Christ and membership in his church is the first step in that eternal life which begins on earth and is continuous with God. Walking in "the way" should be reflected in their day-by-day living and each one, by example, should influence the lives of his associates.

VISITATION

Only the visitation of members by the deacons will be considered in this section. Visitors and the unchurched of the community will be taken up under another heading. There are many aspects of visitation, and a few will be presented to stimulate thought.

A new member should be visited soon after he has received the hand of fellowship. Every visit should have a purpose. The new member is visited to show him that he is a part of the church, to help him to assimilate the church as a vital part of his life, and to aid in his integration into the life of the church. The deacon or deaconess, or both, should make the first visit. Other callers should follow soon thereafter. Each visitor should keep the purpose of the visit uppermost in his mind so that his attention will not be diverted and the call become a mere social visit. Unless new members are already a part of the church life, they find it most difficult to adjust themselves and be accepted into the various groups of the church. The deacons and other callers can speed this orientation and acceptance by their own example and by bringing the new members into active participation in various activities which are appropriate for their particular ages and interests.

There are times when a call should be made by someone other than a member of the diaconate. In order to be ready for such a contingency, the deacons may prepare a list of qualified visitors from the church school and youth groups. In some churches the deacons appoint a "fellowship friend" for each new member, to take care of him for the first year. A full description of the "Fellowship Friend" plan will be found in the Appendix.

Members of longer standing in the church must also be visited by the deacons. A regular schedule of visitation of each member should be drawn up. Every member should be visited two or three times a year if possible, but certainly at least once each year. A definite plan for visitation is imperative so that no one will be overlooked or neglected.

The Zone Visitation Plan is recommended, under which the church's geographical area is divided into zones. For a full description of this plan, see the Appendix.

The purposes of visiting members are numerous and varied, and only a few suggestive ones can be enumerated. Information can be given about the opportunities, aims, and aspirations of the church. Coming events can be announced and explained in detail. Persons in special sorrow or special joy should be visited, for the sorrows or the joys of one member must be the sorrows and joys of the entire church fellowship. Whenever a member has a physical, psychological, mental, or financial need, a visit to provide the needed spiritual or temporal help is necessary. The absence of a member from attendance at the services for an unknown reason demands a prompt visit.

A special kind of visiting is that of bringing the solace of the church to the sick and the aged. Whether the member is temporarily or chronically ill, has suffered a sudden accident or tragedy, is confined to an institution or shut-in his own home, the visitor has the unique privilege of renewing the member's spirit and bringing him good cheer by means of fellowship, reading the Scriptures, prayer, or words of friendship and comfort. Such a visit is the finest way of making the member realize that the church cares about him. And not the least of benefits of visiting, whether of this or any other type, is the enrichment of the deacon's own life.

WELCOMING MEMBERS

Although the importance of the welcoming of members has been covered more fully under the discussion on worship (cf. p. 41), it should be pointed out that the deacons have an excellent opportunity for renewing fellowship and discovering which members may be neglectful by welcoming the people as they arrive and leave the church services. Each deacon should pay particular attention to those members for whom he is responsible.

STEWARDSHIP

Too often, stewardship has come to be regarded as an ironbound requirement to give one-tenth of income for the work of the kingdom. This view comes from a sketchy reading of the Old Testament, which actually requires much more. But the formula of the Old Testament has been superseded by the New Testament teaching that everything we are and have belongs to God. This total obligation has often been summed up in the words "time, talent, and treasure." However stewardship is expressed in words, it is rightly understood only when we recognize that all things, including ourselves, belong to God.

The erroneous conception of stewardship as referring principally to money has allowed the activity to fall into a gray area in the responsibility of the deacon. Thus, the board of trustees, a finance committee, the board of Christian education, or some other group has frequently assumed a part—but only a part—of the work of stewardship. In churches where such a procedure has taken place, the proper emphasis is not put on the share of time and talents which the individual owes to God, who has given all. Neglect of these debts results in inadequate training, or no training at all, and a corresponding dearth of leaders and workers in the church. The deacon should not only be a good steward himself in every sense of the word, but he should lead and inspire others in the fulfillment of this grace.

MISSIONS

Like stewardship, any significant emphasis upon missions often has been forfeited to some other group in the church, or is being neglected. In most churches, the women have carried the burden of the missionary enterprise and are responsible for most of what is accomplished on its behalf. However, no amount of efficiency and energy on the part of the women succeeds in reaching the imagination of all. The deacons must emphasize the mission of the church in the homes as they visit the members.

EVANGELISM

Evangelism is a part of the everyday work of the deacon. When the deacon is visiting, for example, he will have opportunities to witness to non-Christians in the homes. If the church does not have an evangelism committee, the deacons and pastor should plan a program of evangelism each year. Many denominations have specific material for the building of such a program. Capable leaders from the membership, beside deacons, should be enlisted in this activity. (See also Chapter 7.)

SELF-DISCIPLINE

Habits, both bad and good ones alike, take considerable time to form. It goes without saying that each member should be constantly watchful to see that the habits which he is forming are good ones. Stewardship, Bible reading, self-improvement, and a prayer life are illustrative of the habits which the deacon should develop in his own life. By example he can help others to discipline their lives to the end that they might develop these good habits in themselves. As the deacon makes his calls, he can bear witness to what discipline has meant to him.

FELLOWSHIP

A Christian church is, among many other concepts, a fellowship of believers. In a fellowship, each one must love and know all the rest. It is the deacons who should make this possible, by providing opportunities which enable members of the church, new and otherwise, to get acquainted with each other. One way of doing this is the publication of information about each new member, giving his name, address, telephone number, and perhaps some additional information. Another method is the serving of a fellowship dinner. This could be a dinner just for the new members, their fellowship friends, and the deacons, or it could be a dinner for the entire congregation to which the new members are invited as guests.

SMALL GROUPS

Individuals discover that they learn much about themselves, about life, and about their place in the modern world as they converse in small groups. Here, the individual both receives and contributes, and through such interchange learns more about Christ, the Christian way, and specific directions for his own life. Such a group may be oriented about discussion, the Bible, or prayer, but one benefit which is sure to accrue is the advantage of a rich Christian fellowship. The deacons should hold themselves responsible for the formation of groups like these.

COUNSELING

There are some extraordinary occasions in the life of a member when he needs help beyond that which he is able to do for himself. In many instances a deacon will be able to render help, if he knows of the need and it is within his ability to serve. With the increasing pace and pressure of modern living many needs arise in the life of a person which the deacon is not qualified to meet. Such persons should be referred to the pastor, who may then render the needed assistance. Although there is increasing realization that pastors require more training in the area of counseling and steps are being taken to accomplish this, there nevertheless will always be problems with which they will not be qualified to cope. In this case, the person may be referred to a specialist in his area of need.

Some churches maintain organized counseling services, but frequently these consist of having a group of specialists available, to whom the person requiring help is referred. Usually the services rendered by these specialists are not free, but the church serves by bringing together those in need and those who can help. The deacon, in the course of his visiting, has the opportunity of discovering many of those needs while they are forming and before they assume serious proportions. At the same time, he should train himself so that he can serve the people for whom he is responsible with increased ability.

COMMUNION FOR SHUT-INS

In these times, no Christian church escapes having a number of members who are unable to attend the services of the Lord's Supper. Some of these people would like to participate in this memorial service. When they express a desire to do so, a deacon should assist the pastor to bring the communion to them. The observance of this ordinance is a solemn occasion. Only those who want to take the elements should partake. In this spirit, communion should not be taken to shut-ins just because they are confined, but only because they desire and request it. Every effort should be made to convey the idea that a service for the shut-in is a church service; otherwise a privately held service is liable to encourage superstitious worship of the Supper itself.

ASSISTANCE

In many places, the Scriptures treat the subject of helping the needy. Members of the early church pooled their assets, and these were shared as needs arose (cf. Acts 2: 44, 45; Acts 4:34, 35). Some other references: 1 John 3:17 (brother in need); Matt. 19:21 (give to the poor); Matt. 25:35-45 (sharing with the needy). This spirit has continued through the history of the Christian church. Today, the churches band together to do the work of assistance on a broader scale, both denominational and interdenominational. Much help for the needy has been taken over by charity organizations, welfare groups, and municipal, state, and federal government agencies, but the Christian church led the way.

In spite of these vast changes in the ways of helping the

needy, there is still, within the fellowship of the local church, much occasion to help those whose needs cannot be met by existing organizations or who would not seek assistance from such charities. To help these people the fellowship fund exists and is used. The needs which occur may take many forms, and prayerful consideration is required before reaching a decision in any situation. The assistance given might be in the form of a cash gift; as a loan with either a specified or an indefinite agreement for repayment; payment of an outstanding bill or bills; food, fuel, or clothing; arranging with a local merchant for limited credit; or finding employment for the needy person. It should be kept in mind that needs are not only financial and physical, but may, instead, be mental and spiritual. Therefore the interpretation of the word "needy" should be most liberal and the deacons should use every opportunity to satisfy every kind of need.

How far the board of deacons can or should go in rendering assistance is a problem which probably has as many solutions as there are local churches. Of course, no more cash assistance can be given than is available in the fellowship fund. If the calls on the fund are excessive, an occasional special appeal can be made to the church to increase the giving. When needs are explained, church members invariably respond. The board of deacons must decide the form which assistance should take in each individual case, as well as the amount of such help, and for how long it should be given. A policy must be established as to whether assistance is to be confined to the members of the church or extended to other needy ones, such as members of other churches, persons who are non-Christians, and the inevitable transients seeking help. In any event, it should be a cardinal rule that assistance is confidential, not a subject of conversation outside of the board meeting, even with the wives and family of the deacons.

The money given into the fellowship fund should never be used for any other purpose except for the needy. In some special instance the church may authorize the use of some of this money for a special purpose. Many churches give the fellowship offering for one month of the year to their pension boards for assistance to such retired ministers and missionaries as are not eligible for a pension or whose pension is too small for the most meager sustenance living. This practice is commendable.

Under no circumstances, however, should the fellowship fund be used for the expenses of the church or for missionary work. Any attempted violation of this principle should be stoutly resisted by the board of deacons on the basis that it would betray the trust of those who gave the money for a specific purpose.

REVIEW MEMBERSHIP ROLL

The task of maintaining an up-to-date and accurate membership roll is not easy, but it should be done thoroughly. As a rule, the rolls should be reviewed annually. Because of the difficulty in locating members who have not attended for some time, the work required to make the contacts and the fear of unfavorable reactions among relatives and friends of the missing members combine to discourage the board of deacons from undertaking this work. Nevertheless, it is absolutely essential to a healthy and functioning church. The review should be made to determine attendance, interest, participation, and support, with the hope of reactivating those members who have been neglectful of their Christian faith and their church. The purpose is to develop a church in which every member is an active, supporting, and witnessing Christian. The method of approach may vary according to the size, situation, and age of the church, the time elapsed since such a review was undertaken, and the sincerity behind the desire to have the membership rolls reflect the actual church membership. In no case should those who are *unable* to attend, participate, or support because of infirmity, illness, inadequate income, or other cause be included when the review is made.

The program used by one church in making a review is discussed. It will illustrate one approach to this problem. First, every person in attendance at the worship services over a period of time was requested to sign a record-of-attendance card. The cards of visitors provided leads for visits by the pastor and deacons; the attendance of members was recorded on a permanent record.

Second, after a year, the records were examined to discover those for whom no attendance was recorded (excepting those who were unable to attend). These were separated into two categories: those who resided within commuting distance and those who lived too far away from the church to be expected to attend. Two letters were sent to people who lived within commuting distance. *The results:* The church learned that some had made connection with other churches and that two wanted their names removed without giving a specific reason.

The members who lived too far from the church to be expected to attend the services regularly were sent a different type of letter, in which they were encouraged to take their memberships to churches in their own communities. A specific church was suggested to each one. Another letter was sent to the pastor of that church, giving the name and address of the member. Both letters mentioned that a letter was also sent to the other person. *The results:* One unknown death was discovered; several united with the recommended church; many had already made connection with other churches without having notified their previous church; and a very few wanted to retain their membership. It was suspected that those who desired to maintain their connection did so for sentimental reasons, instead of the practical Christian attitude of serving and supporting a church which they could attend. (Sample letters are shown in the Appendix.)

Third, the area was marked out in geographical zones, including all within commuting distance, and two deacons were assigned to each zone. With this method there should not be any members withdrawing from active participation in the church life unless a deacon is aware of it. Thus, steps can be taken at once to restore such persons before they drift so far away that they cannot be reached.

After one thoroughgoing review has been made, succeeding annual reviews should entail much less work, provided the deacons are constantly fulfilling their responsibilities of visiting and watchcare. The purpose which the deacon should always keep uppermost in his mind and heart is to have every member of the church an active, supporting, and witnessing follower of Christ. Removal of a name from the church roll should be the last resort; but when a person has indicated no interest and does not attend, the removal of his name is no more than a recognition that he has already removed himself, and merely confirms his act.

DISCIPLINE

There is probably no deacon in any church who hears or reads this section but who wishes that there might be no such word as "discipline" in the Christian's vocabulary. However, wishing will not change the nature of man, and there will always be some who are in need of discipline. It is often true that those who strive to lead their lives according to the teachings of Christ are lacking in self-discipline and are buffeted by Satan and the forces of evil which are ever at work. The unpleasantness of imposing disciplinary action upon a fellow Christian tends to discourage any movement in this direction, but the need is often apparent. We note this need even in the early church, for Paul writes: "Brethren, if a man is overtaken in any trespass, you who are spiritual should restore him in a spirit of gentleness. Look to yourself, lest you too be tempted" (Gal. 6:1). Implied in Paul's prescription is that any disciplinary action must be done in love and with understanding.

Two general kinds of offenders are objects of discipline: (1) Those who have committed acts unbecoming a Christian, and (2) Those who have been neglectful of their Christian calling. Those in the first category, it may be pointed out, will include those who engage in malicious gossip or talk which tends to disrupt the fellowship. These and all others who have conducted themselves in a manner unbecoming a Christian are in apparent need of discipline.

Neglect which requires discipline is less clearly defined. When the deacons should take action and how they should proceed cannot be given pat answers. Individuals and situations differ so widely that only some general principles can be outlined. It is necessary, first, to ascertain the reasons behind the neglect and, further, to find out whether they are justified, based on a misunderstanding, or are merely an excuse. If they are justified, the deacons should try to eliminate whatever is the harmful element in the life of the church. If they are the result of misunderstanding, the deacons will bring the facts to light. In any case, every cause for friction must be examined, to the end that there be no valid reason for an individual to neglect his church and his Christ.

If the neglect on the part of a member takes the form of his failure to support the worship services or the work of the church, or both, a visit may reveal the reasons. In most instances it will be discovered that the real cause of the member's neglect is to be found within himself, and is a loss of that spiritual vitality which can come only from the working of the Holy Spirit in his life. Without this power, indifference and neglect of the spiritual aspects of life develop. Such people often claim that they want to see their church grow and advance, but at the same time they fail to participate so that such growth and advancement can come about. Their failure to help not only retards advancement but their bad example becomes the cause for others also to withhold their participation, and the church suffers doubly. It is most difficult to persuade these reluctant ones to renew their interest.

Compulsory attendance at training classes before membership is one way to forestall this indifference and neglect. At this early time, the new member can be nurtured until the indwelling of the Holy Spirit has become a part of his way of life. Only those who have had a real encounter with Him should be admitted to membership.

HELPING THE PASTOR

In either a large or a small church, the responsibilities of the pastor are often difficult and disagreeable. Anything the deacons can do to help him, either in the performance of such tasks or in upholding him in prayer to show him that he has the support and backing of his closest associates, will help him to bear these heavy burdens. The pastor should be able to depend upon the deacons.

Decisions must constantly be made by the pastor. Herein, the support and counsel of the deacons are invaluable. Wise deacons will offer these humbly, so that the pastor's decisions may be made with added wisdom and understanding. The deacons should make it easy for the pastor to approach them.

Pastors, like laymen, vary in their personalities, individualisms, and idiosyncrasies. Nonetheless, there should be a close fellowship between the deacons and the pastor. Such particulars as mannerisms in the pulpit, methods of preaching, and habits of visitation will vary among pastors and sometimes the deacons (and congregation) feel an unhappy urge to try to remake the pastor to conform to their own ideas or to imitate some predecessor.

Even when the pastor exerts the utmost kindness and consideration, he may unwittingly injure the feeling of some member or do something which offends the members. If such a thing happens, the deacons should feel free to have a frank discussion with the pastor, to make him aware of the problem and help him to bring about a better situation or explain the purpose behind his action. In most instances the atmosphere will be cleared when motives are understood by all concerned. The deacons must always hold themselves responsible for helping to maintain proper relationships between pastor and people.

Through long usage, we have come to think of watchcare as a process in which the pastor, and sometimes the board of deacons, maintains a vigilance over the members of the church. But it is also true that the pastor himself is a member, and, as a human being, has needs of his own. The board of deacons and each individual deacon should be aware of this, with the aim of maintaining a close, Christian relationship with the pastor. Such a spiritual bond becomes the core for complete Christian fellowship throughout the church, the climate wherein the Spirit can perform his work in individuals and church alike.

IMPLEMENTATION

The framework of the organization of the board of deacons should be revised from time to time, but all such changes should make the board a vital and functioning arm of the church. It can well be questioned whether any group can do all of the things that have been suggested in these pages, but it is certain that plans must be developed and a start made. Meetings and discussions will reveal needs, but the work will be accomplished only by making a start on some portion of the work, the extent of which will depend on the number of deacons who consecrate themselves to the task and give the necessary time to the accomplishment of the job.

Planning should be done carefully, thoughtfully, and prayerfully, in the knowledge that the better the plans and organization the more fruitful the result. But one would be like an ostrich hiding its head in the sand to believe that a well organized board is the total answer. People are not won to Christ and encouraged to continue in his way by slick organization, but by convicted persons working effectively under the guidance of the Holy Spirit. The watchcare committee of the board of deacons should see that all of the deacons are taking care of the members for whom they are responsible and, if other persons are assisting, that they too are measuring up to their tasks.

SUMMARY

Watchcare is a constant concern for the total life of the members. And the church should minister to the whole person. This concern should cause the deacon to be as much involved in the life of the members as in the life of his own family. Anything which tends to prevent or disrupt harmony within the fellowship is an opportunity for him to promote accord and prevent differences among the members from becoming sources of prolonged discord and strife. All functions of the deacon meet in the focal point of helping the members to grow and function as new persons in Christ.

QUESTIONS FOR DISCUSSION

1. Occasionally a new member complains that the church pays less attention to him than it did before he became a member. Assuming that there is some truth in this charge, what is the responsibility of the deacons in this area?

2. Think back to the time when you first joined the church, and comment on the help you received in getting to know the people and program of the church.

3. Discuss the comparative advantage of caring for the needs of individuals by visitation and by letter.

7

THE UNCHURCHED

A SIGNIFICANT PART OF THE WORK of the deacon is the concentration upon those who have never made a commitment to Christ and those who have become separated from him, and are, accordingly, outside the fellowship of the church. As many as possible of such people should be discovered, led to Christ, trained, and brought into the church membership.

DISCOVERING THE UNCHURCHED

It goes without saying that any deacon will extend a greeting to all who come to worship. But special attention should be paid to those who are unchurched, for they have already expressed their interest by making the first move. To be sure, some visitors attending the services are transients, in which case the pastor may send them a letter, but there are enough of those who are not transients to make this group a fruitful source. An effort should be made to ascertain the names and addresses of all visitors by such means as a visitors' register in the narthex, attendance cards in the pews, or discreet questions by the pastor and deacons.

Another group of likely prospects exists inherently in

every church fellowship. This group consists of relatives and friends of active members. These people already know something about the local church and its pastor, and often many of them are waiting to be approached in an official manner.

Beyond, but not excluding the groups mentioned above, there are vast numbers of people in every community who have never had a conversion experience and are not connected with any church. Moreover, there are those who once belonged to a church but whose membership, for one reason or another, has ceased to exist. In these days of shifting population, families are frequently moving into the neighborhood, and these new arrivals vary in their interest and attitudes toward the church as widely as any others.

The church school, youth groups, and various other organizations and societies connected with the church or using the church's facilities provide continuing sources for the discovery of prospects. These organizations embrace many who are not members of the church or who are just reaching the age when they are eligible for membership.

There are certain techniques for discovering prospects early and efficiently. A door-to-door canvass of the community or of newly-occupied houses can be made. Often such a canvass is made in cooperation with other churches in the area, but sometimes is done by a single church. Some communities have a welcome wagon, wherein a representative calls upon newcomers and points out the advantages and services of the community. Part of the work of this representative is to ascertain the religious affiliation of the newcomers and refer their names to the corresponding church. Realtors and utilities such as the electric company are often, though not invariably, found to be cooperative in helping a church to be informed when houses become occupied. The members of the church should always be on the alert for new neighbors, and should report them to the pastor and deacons immediately.

VISITING PROSPECTS

In every church, a list or file of prospects should be organized and maintained. The pastor or chairman of the board should then assign the names of prospects to the members of the board, and visitations should be made within a few days. These visits should have the purpose of ultimately bringing people into a happy and active relationship with Christ and the church.

TESTING CANDIDATES

Because the decision to join the church is the most important action which can be taken by the candidate, it is necessary that this step be taken in complete realization of its importance. In light of this, the deacons should test the sincerity of the candidate and discover as far as humanly possible his desire to live in the Christian way. All such interviewing should be done in a loving, understanding spirit so that God can work in both the candidate and the deacons.

In the case of those who are making a decision for the first time, as, for example, those who have responded to an invitation given during a church service or an evangelistic meeting, the questions should be so framed as to elicit whether or not the candidate has had a real experience with Christ and an understanding of what is involved in making this decision. The age of the candidate will be a factor in the framing of the questions and the answers which can be expected.

As one of the greatest sources of candidates is the church school, some persons who are immature may be coming for admission into membership in the church without realizing the seriousness of the step which they are taking. This is especially applicable with children who are group conscious and may be moved more by their fellowship with one another than by the Holy Spirit. Some weeding out will be done by the pastor before submitting them to the deacons, but if further questioning indicates that a candidate is not yet ready for admittance, it is essential for the deacons to explain to him the reason. An interview with the parents also of a child or youth is advisable so that they too may be made aware of the reason. A situation like this will demand the deepest Christian love and tact on the part of the deacons, the candidate, and the parents, so that God's will may be accomplished in the life of the candidate.

If the candidate should be coming from another church of similar faith and order, the questions should be geared to obtain information regarding his previous Christian experience and service. A letter of commendation should be requested from the church of which the candidate is a member, describing the standing of the candidate and confirming his service in that church.

When the situation is that a candidate has been out of touch with his church or his church has closed, the questions should be directed towards testing the reality of his experience, or the change which has occurred in his life, and his present sincerity. Such candidates are said to be received on experience.

The questions directed to candidates from churches of other denominations should aim to gain a knowledge of their previous Christian experience. Among other things the candidate should give his reason for abandoning his present denominational affiliation. It is also necessary that he shall understand and accept the beliefs and practices of the church he is about to join. Moreover, if his former membership was in any evangelical church, a letter of commendation from that church should be forthcoming.

INSTRUCTION OF CANDIDATES

Discipleship classes are an effective aid in the church training program. They supplement the work of the church school and make it possible to discover the sincerity of the candidate's profession of faith. They are the means whereby the candidate learns what the acceptance of Christ involves in his life, the meaning of church membership, the church's beliefs and practices, and the outreach of the church.

It is often said that all candidates for membership, without exception, should be required to attend a discipleship class. Any class should be composed of people whose experience and backgrounds are similar, and, as far as possible, there should be a separate class for each age group. The number of sessions and the content may vary with the age and the experience of the group, at the discretion of the pastor. Classes for children may be held on weekday afternoons after school, while those for adults and young people might be held during the church school sessions, in the evening, or Sunday afternoons. It is helpful to the candidate if he is able to complete his attendance at the discipleship class prior to appearing before the deacons, so the deacons may make a recommendation to church following the interview. He is then better prepared to answer questions and state his convictions, and the deacons have a more basic understanding upon which to make their recommendations to the church. Some denominations publish graded discipleship texts, available from the denomination's bookstore or its state or national headquarters.

Leadership of a discipleship class is generally provided by the pastor. However, an assistant or associate pastor, a director of Christian education, or a qualified deacon can be used in this capacity under the direction and supervision of the pastor. There may be times when more than one class is needed because of the different age groups and it is helpful when another leader is available. At least one pastor has preached a series of sermons on the subjects generally considered in discipleship classes. Such use of the Sunday morning worship service serves as a refresher course for every member, as well as a training class for those who are seeking membership. The use of the sermon in this way offers the bonus of conserving the pastor's time. But there is also a weakness in this procedure, for there are those who will absent themselves from the services because of the special sermon topics. The Sunday morning congregation is not a captive one. The deacons and pastor should consider all possible effects, good and bad, of the training sermon. However, the success or failure of the plan, as with any new idea, can be determined only by trying it.

The deacons share with the pastor in making certain that all candidates are well prepared for practicing the new life as a follower of Christ and assuming a place in the life of the church and its work. Each candidate should become well informed about the meaning of church membership, the obligations and responsibilities of members, the functions of the church, and the organization of the church and all its related groups. The responsibility for follow-up belongs to the watchcare committee.

In many cases, churches provide for an evangelism committee which is responsible for planning, initiating, and co-ordinating the evangelistic program of the church. However, a committee for evangelism generally orginates because the deacons have not been active in this area. Where such a committee is functioning, the deacons should assist it.

Evangelism is *the* work of the church. It is not a mere side issue, to be found in certain programs, necessary as programs may be. Rather, evangelism takes place as the Holy Spirit works in and through consecrated Christians and groups of Christians. Nothing could be more important in the work of a deacon than the reaching of those who do not know the one God and his Son, Jesus Christ, as Savior and do not experience the joy of serving under the guidance of the Holy Spirit.

The inefficacy of the Christian church to grow satisfactorily in numbers and spirit probably stems from the failure of Christians (who are *the church*) to consider evangelism as the fundamental responsibility of each Christian. The deacons should be the first to acknowledge this responsibility. Above all, they should be evangelists for Christ, setting the example for others.

Back of this apparent lack of interest in personal witnessing there may be a lack of knowledge and technical skill. Although the average Christian receives training for many years in a knowledge of the Bible and the working of God, Christ, and the Holy Spirit in the lives of the disciples, he seems to receive insufficient discipline in spreading the good news. We must not forget that the disciples were with Jesus for many months learning to be fishers of men. Even with such preparation, they were not permitted to go out as evangelists until they were empowered by the Holy Spirit.

Any church member must be taught how to be an evangelist as he must be taught how to perform any other task. Some rare individuals may learn without any training, and some may be informally tutored by a friend who is interested in helping them to become evangelists. Should we expect a person to feel adequate to do this work if he has not been trained? It is not surprising that the average Christian feels unqualified to speak to others about their souls' salvation.

Person-to-person visitation to win others for Christ is essential. The shepherd does not increase his flock; it is sheep who reproduce sheep to make the flock grow. Jesus Christ, the Good Shepherd, expects the people of his church to meet and evangelize other people that his flock may grow. In the home, in the factory or office, in the school, in the church and its organizations, and anywhere in life's contacts Christians should tell others about Jesus Christ.

No Christian should forego the thrill of witnessing to

others of what Christ has meant to him in his life, and of how great is the joy of the Christian life. Such witnessing is the sowing of the seed or the watering of seed already sown, in the confidence that the results are in the hands of God and that the Holy Spirit can fulfill the task of developing the seed until it bears fruit.

QUESTIONS FOR DISCUSSION

1. In addition to the methods described in this book, how can the deacons discover prospective church members?

2. What are some of the questions the deacons should ask candidates for membership? Should the questions always be identical for all candidates?

3. What obligation to participate in the work of evangelism does the new member have? Do the deacons have any leadership responsibility in this respect?

8

TRAINING

ONE OF THE INSTRUCTIONS which Paul gave to Timothy regarding deacons was: "Let them also be tested first; then if they prove themselves blameless let them serve as deacons" (1 Tim. 3:10). This means that the church should select as deacons those members who show by their lives that they are redeemed persons. But it is a well-known fact that many people who are newly elected do not know what their responsibilities are going to be, nor how to perform them.

Personnel for many occupations and professions are first given field training, internship, or "on-the-job" training. During the period of such training the problems which are encountered help the individual to become adjusted gradually, and avoid the shock which would otherwise accompany the sudden change from rosy theoretical concepts to harsh realities. Individuals often enter into a field of endeavor only to become disillusioned when they are confronted with the demands of their situations. The newly elected deacon is no exception to this liability to disillusionment.

If any church is to function efficiently for success in its

mission, it must be guided by trained leaders in addition to the pastor. Opportunities for such training should be provided for all leaders in the church. A regularly scheduled training course for deacons is especially useful. Thus they can improve themselves and increase the extent and quality of their service.

While very few churches make it mandatory for their leaders to take one or more training courses as a requisite for holding office, some do so in the case of their church school teachers. Yet, the opportunity should be given not only to teachers, but to all leaders, to participate voluntarily in training courses and classes, which should be offered on a planned and continuing basis. This applies especially to the deacons, who, as the leaders of leaders, should seize every opportunity to find better ways in which to serve both church and community.

METHODS OF TRAINING

Most local churches would find it awkward to presume to train their deacons, because of the personalities involved. To overcome this plight, a group of churches or an association can offer training courses or classes for deacons without encountering such a problem. Such classes would enable the church to train prospective deacons or young people who may become deacons in the future and thus provide for trained workers available to assume office. The practice of training in advance is especially important and beneficial when church policy dictates a limited term in office resulting in rotation of personnel.

There are churches that have "junior deacons." A junior

deacon is generally a young person who is a member of the church and who shows great promise as a church worker. The responsibilities placed upon a junior deacon are less than those placed upon a mature deacon. Moreover, the training and experience which can be given to a junior deacon are considered to be efficient planning to provide a pool of possible trained deacons for the future. It should be pointed out, however, that there are many who oppose the formal setting-up of a board or group of junior deacons, despite the apparent opportunities for giving them training and experience. Those who object to the practice claim that it brands the junior deacon as a kind of second-class member of the church who is not yet eligible to be elected to the most important offices. There is nothing in the Scriptures to support the idea of the junior deacon.

One of the miracles which God has worked in the church has been the progress which has been made despite the lack of trained deacons. Of course, much of this advance has been possible because other groups of interested and committed persons have taken over certain tasks which rightfully are within the province of the deacons. Thus there have grown up the established board of trustees, board of Christian education, board of missionary promotion, evangelism committee, stewardship committee, Christian friendliness committee, Christian social concern committee, and many others. Where many boards and committees now exist in a local church, the deacons can give their encouragement and cooperation, and the deacons can perform services not presently being covered by any group. But the time has come for deacons to realize the full extent of their responsibilities, train themselves for these and other greater tasks, recommit their lives to God, and assume all of the obligations of their office.

QUESTIONS FOR DISCUSSION

1. How can individuals be trained in the work of the deacon before they are chosen to be deacons?

2. Should previous training be required before one is eligible to serve as a deacon? Why?

3. What criteria (such as age, sex, spiritual development) should be used in the selection of trainees?

4. Under what circumstances should the church's youth be invited to observe a meeting of the board of deacons? Name some benefits and some disadvantages.

9

RELATIONSHIPS

THERE IS NOT MUCH OF A PROBLEM concerning interorganizational relationships in those churches in which the board of deacons is responsible for the major portion of the work. However, churches which have many specialized organizations and groups are handicapped with a source of duplication of effort and misunderstanding. Close cooperation and much toleration are required.

Many churches have an advisory council or board or other group especially formed for the purpose of providing over-all coordination, but this neither relieves nor excuses the deacons from performing the duties which rightfully belong to them. Some of the ways in which the board of deacons must cooperate with others for the utmost efficiency and performance of the most effective work in the church are listed. Obviously, when the work is already being well done, the deacons should refrain from all interference.

Board of trustees
    Formation of budget
    Use of building
    Approval of program

Board of Christian education

Get every member involved in some task

Make use of every talent in the church

Obtain efficient use of all available manpower

Help to train leaders

If there is no board, work with the church school superintendent and others

Board of missionary promotion

Assist in program

Assist in educating church members in stewardship

Evangelism committee

Assist in program

Work with committee members in visitation

Advisory or planning board; committee; council

Provide leadership on board

Be example in interest and work

Submit plans and suggestions

Be an influence for true fellowship and cooperation

Give direction and inspiration—help to eliminate listlessness and drifting

Pastor

He cannot be a one-man army. Give him the support he needs in good works

He will not be perfect. Criticize when necessary, but be sympathetic and kind

Pray for him

Help to make him feel secure; Good salary, pension, vacation. See that your present pastor is treated as well as you would be forced to treat a new one

Choirs
   Have prayer with them
   Watch their deportment during worship services

Ushers
   Give guidance for the best ushering service
   Help in ushering as needed

Decorating or flower committee
   Make suggestions, especially for special seasons or
      events
   Assist if needed

COOPERATION WITH PULPIT COMMITTEE

When a vacancy in the pulpit occurs, it is of prime concern to the deacons that the man whom God has selected to serve the church be found. As individuals and as a board, the deacons should frequently be in prayer for God's leadership in obtaining a pastor. Occasionally the board of deacons becomes the pulpit committee of the church, but usually only one or two deacons serve on such a committee, along with representatives of other boards, committees, organizations, and the church at large. However the procedure for the settling of a pastor is ordered, the deacons should hold themselves ready to provide leadership. To be sure, some pulpit committees perform their work so privately and secretly that not even the deacons know what is being done, but when this is the case, the wisdom and experience of the deacons are being wasted. A more efficient and wiser course is to expect the deacons to lead in seeking the aid of the Holy Spirit in the matter. In a peculiar way, unavailable to any other group in the church, the deacons will be able to inform the pulpit committee of problems and difficulties in the church life, so that there may be frank discussion of them with the prospective pastor. If this candidate is the right man for the church, these difficult situations will not discourage him, but will challenge him to seek guidance and strength in advance.

After a minister has accepted the invitation of the church to become its pastor, two events should be planned: the installation of the new pastor and a reception for the pastor and his family. The church must decide who shall plan these occasions. Sometimes one or both of them are made the responsibility of the board of deacons.

An installation service should be discussed with the pastor so that the participants are those whom he desires from among his friends, former pastors, professors, and representatives from the association and conventions. Such deference to the wishes of the pastor is most appropriate, for the service is in his honor. If the deacons are called upon to help arrange the program, they should concur heartily with the pastor's wishes and suggestions.

The reception for the pastor and his family is a pleasant event whose very nature requires that it be planned by the people of the church. Sometimes it follows the installation service immediately, but if such a service is on a Sunday it may be preferable to separate the two events, and hold the reception on a weekday evening, and perhaps after a midweek service. The church-designated group responsible for the reception should arrange for the program by completely providing for speakers, entertainment, refreshments, and any other components of the reception.

The installation of the pastor and the reception for him and his family do not consummate the relationship between pastor and deacons. On the contrary, the relationship is then only in its infancy. The deacons can do much to help the new pastor become established and to maintain a happy and productive relationship throughout his entire time with the church.

QUESTIONS FOR DISCUSSION

1. If two groups want to schedule events which would compete for participants or space, what action should the deacons take?

2. If ushers are inclined to wear clothing which the deacons feel is unsuitable, what action should the deacons take?

3. What other conflicts between groups in the church should receive the attention of the deacons?

4. In cases where there is an overlapping of areas of work (for example, work by the Women's Fellowship and by the Board of Missions), should the board of deacons mediate or remain aloof?

10

FINANCES

WHAT SHOULD BE THE EXTENT of the deacons' interest in and occupation with the financial affairs of the church? There are those who erroneously believe that the work of the deacon should be narrowly confined to that which they consider to be "spiritual." Such people overlook the spiritual implications in almost every facet of life and church procedures. As God is interested in everything we think and do, so must the church and its deacons be similarly interested. Those who take the opposite viewpoint, claiming that everything has spiritual significance, are probably nearer the truth. That there is a place in the work of the deacon for an emphasis upon the financial phase of the Christian life cannot be questioned.

In states where the law does not require a church to have trustees, the board of deacons sometimes forms a committee to manage all financial affairs and property of the church. Even in states with laws requiring trustees, it is frequently the policy of a church to elect a number of deacons to serve as the board of trustees. This plan of organization has much to commend it because it tends to maintain the level of the spiritual life of all officers of the church at the high standards of the deacons. Another advantage is that all phases of work—finances, education, worship, missions, evangelism, and others—are closely woven together in purpose and goals.

One of the more usual ways of organizing a church is that of having separate groups responsible for each major phase of work. This puts finances and property into the hands of a board of trustees. But even in churches which are so constituted, the board of deacons has a definite responsibility for some of the financial areas of the church work.

SPIRITUAL BUSINESS MEN

Many deacons are business men who know the importance of money and are capable of handling it. Also, deacons are more conscious than the average member of needs in the wider fields of service, local, home missions, and foreign missions. They are apt to be familiar with the way in which associations and conventions play their part through the money received from the local churches. The deacons are in a position to explain the relationship between the local church and these larger organizations, and they can do much to encourage giving for these needs as well as the needs of the local church.

The deacon, more than anyone else, recognizes that each person's money and possessions are only a trust. The deacons know that giving by the individual is indicative of his spiritual development, judging not so much by the amount but rather by the spirit of the giving. Jesus, watching at the temple, gave his judgment of giving by the people and stressed the value of sacrificial giving. The deacon can set an example in sacrificial giving as well as talk about it. The average Christian is prone to forget that everything he has belongs to God and it is the deacon's responsibility to remind him of this fact and that every Christian has a duty to practice good stewardship. Anything worthwhile will cost something. Emphasis must be on giving without expectation of financial reward. Financial reward may come, but the greatest reward will be in spiritual enrichment.

DEACONS AND THE PROPERTY

In those churches where the deacons are responsible for the finances and property of the church, they are responsible also for the use of the building as well as for its upkeep. To grant the use of the building for stated services and the responsible organizations of the church is usually a mere formality, but social and fund-raising activities require close scrutiny to determine whether or not they are appropriate or desirable. This writer feels that fund-raising events should not be allowed in any church, because of the nature of the church; but, even if there is an inclination to permit them, consideration should be given to the adverse effect they may have on local merchants of the community who are at a disadvantage in competing with a tax-exempt church with no overhead.

Sometimes groups other than those closely affiliated with the church may request the use of the building. Each such request should be thoroughly checked as to its purpose, program, and the portion of the building which is required. Most of these requests will come from Christian groups, such as leadership education schools and association or convention meetings; but others may come from groups which are outside the Christian fellowship. When plans are being formulated for secular shows, the deacons should review the script before approving the use of the building.

The deacons are the responsible body for making such decisions. This means that the pastor is completely relieved from making them. Thus, the board, not the pastor, can bear the brunt of any dissatisfaction or criticism.

In churches which have a separate board of trustees, the trustees will assume much responsibility for the uses of the buildings, but the board of deacons should be required to examine the purpose and program of these events, and enabled to withhold the use of the property if the proposed use does not meet the church's standards. The important thing for the deacons to bear in mind is that the entire church building, including the sanctuary, the church school rooms, and the social hall, is the house of God, dedicated to the work of his kingdom.

QUESTIONS FOR DISCUSSION

1. In some churches a new member is handed a package of offering envelopes, including a pledge card, without comment and without any previous membership training. What is the responsibility of the deacons in such a situation?

2. If the church is opposed to fund-raising activities by policy or tradition, what should the board of deacons do about a group which suddenly decides to institute a benefit fund-raising activity?

11

THE DEACONESS

THE IDEA OF THE DEACONESS is not new. There were deaconesses in the New Testament church, in the churches of the first several centuries, and there are deaconesses in today's churches. However, there are questions concerning the place of the deaconess in the work of the church which are not always easily answered, and which, therefore, are answered in different ways. Is a deaconess a feminine deacon? Does she have the same duties as those of a deacon? Is she to be prohibited from exercising any of the duties commonly performed by deacons? Is she charged with special responsibilities that are outside the province of the deacon? Is her status lower or higher than that of a deacon? Should there be a separate board of deaconesses?

ORIGIN

In the New Testament church, when seven individuals were chosen to minister to widows and serve tables, all of them were men (cf. Acts 6:1-6). Nevertheless, the New Testament does record the presence of women workers in the churches. Paul wrote to the church at Philippi: "Help these women, for they have labored side by side with me in the gospel. . ." (Phil. 4:3). In the letter to the Romans Paul wrote: "I commend to you our sister Phoebe, a deaconess of the church at Cenchreae, that you may . . . help her in whatever she may require of you, for she has been a helper of many and of myself as well" (Rom. 16:1-2). These references imply that many, if not all, early churches had in them women who served and were called deaconesses.

During the first five Christian centuries, there was a document called the Apostolic Constitutions, which offered instruction in church discipline, worship, and doctrine. This was not authoritative, and was never used by all of the churches, but it does give us a glimpse into some of the thinking about deaconesses during those early centuries. Some of the functions of a deaconess named in this document are as follows: She was to be ordained for the ministrations toward women. She was called the assistant or minister to the deacon. She was to perform certain duties which deacons were expressly ordered not to perform. She sometimes assisted the presbyter at the baptism of women. She was to stand at the entrance to the church to greet the women, show them to their seats, and maintain order among them. Among the limitations prescribed in the document upon the duties of the deaconess were the prohibition for her to serve at the altar, to teach, to baptize, or in any way perform any of the functions of the clergy.

The deaconess was recognized in the councils of Nicaea, 325, and Chalcedon, 451, but some later councils rejected the institution, and it was virtually discontinued in the middle ages by the Christian church.

In modern times the creation of deaconesses has been revived. In 1833, Pastor Theodor Fliedner organized an order of deaconesses particularly to train nurses for hospital work at Kaiserwerth, Westphalia. This order soon assumed the general duties of teaching and parish work. In 1862, Bishop Archibald Campbell Tait of London set apart Miss Elizabeth Ferard as a deaconess in the Church of England, and other dioceses adopted the practice. It soon became common in Lutheran, Presbyterian, and Methodist churches, as well as in the Anglican.

There are two main streams of thought regarding the status of the deaconess today. One of these holds that the deaconess is a deacon. As such, she possesses all the requisites, qualifications, and training, and carries on all of the functions of a deacon. The second view is that the status of a deaconess is different from that of a deacon. Under this view, her duties vary from those of the deacon, and, like the duties of those in the early centuries, are concentrated upon the needs of the women in the church.

Prejudice exists in some churches against having deaconesses. Members of such churches cite such passages as: "Let a woman learn in silence with all submissiveness. I permit no woman to teach or to have authority over men" (1 Tim. 2:11-12). But permitting the interpretation of an isolated passage of Scripture to prevent employment of women in today's church seems to be open to criticism. A church which uses this Scripture passage as a reason for not having deaconesses might logically be persuaded to exclude women as church school teachers, youth counselors, or from other responsible offices.

It should be taken into account that Paul praised the women in many others of his letters. He made no distinction in sex when he wrote to the churches at Rome (cf. Rom. 12:1-8) and Corinth (cf. 1 Cor. 12:1-31) about the gifts which have been given, the service to be expected, and the oneness of the church as the body of Christ. It appears to be inconceivable that Paul would exclude all the women of the church when he said, "You are the body of Christ and individually members of it" (1 Cor. 12:27). It is recommended that churches which do not have a board of deaconesses, or a board of deacons made up of both men and women, give thoughtful, prayerful consideration to a change of policy so that they may take advantage of the contributions which women can make in this important area of the church's work and witness.

REQUISITES

Paul wrote to the Galatian Christians: "For as many of you as were baptized into Christ have put on Christ. There is neither Jew nor Greek, there is neither slave nor free, there is neither male nor female; for you are all one in Christ Jesus" (Gal. 3:27-28). Considering that in Christ there is neither male nor female, and recognizing the high status of women in today's world, it follows that the requisites of the deacon apply equally to the deaconess.

QUALIFICATIONS

Everything in Chapter 2 regarding the qualifications which should be possessed by a deacon applies equally to a deaconess, allowing, of course, for the natural difference between the sexes. One further word of caution may be in order. There are those who are inclined to accuse women of frequently bending to idle words, gossip, and slander. Whether or not their accusation is true is beside the point. The fact that such things are said and believed by some people makes it imperative that a woman who holds a high position in the church be especially guarded in her conversation. Men and women alike should recall the admonition that the tongue is tremendously powerful (cf. James 3:1-12).

ORGANIZATION

The general principles outlined in Chapter 3 apply to the organization of deaconesses. Concepts of the status and work of the deaconess vary from church to church, however, and modification of the structure may become necessary to meet the requirements of any given church. Each church will decide what its policy shall be, but there are some considerations to be evaluated.

Some churches prefer to have a separate board of deaconesses. When this is the case, the boards of deacons and deaconesses hold separate meetings in some churches, while in other churches they meet together. Because of the extremely close relationship which exists between the deacons and the pastor, his presence is almost a necessity. When there are two separate meetings, the pastor must, or at least should, attend both meetings. If both are on the same evening he is obliged to divide his time between the boards. In separate meetings, a lack of coordination (if not cooperation) may exist as each board discusses and acts upon the matters which come before it. Even when the boards are cooperative, matters may be delayed until a basis for action is developed. The pastor will serve as liaison between the boards, of course, but nevertheless there will be delays which may hinder the work. Joint meetings of the boards held at regular intervals provide another partial solution to this problem.

Some churches have one board of deacons, which consists of both men and women. Such churches may use the term "deacon" for all members of the board, men and women alike, in recognition that their service and status are identical. Many of the disadvantages of maintaining two separate boards are automatically solved by this form of organization.

The number of women elected to serve, compared to the number of men, is often a question to be decided by the church. It may be that the church prefers not to make any rule. Some churches provide for an equal number of men and women. Other churches choose to have fewer women than men, on the premise that the women have less work to perform. Equal numbers permit equal assignment to zones of the parish and to positions on various committees of the board or boards. Unequal numbers suggest that those in the minority have not been given adequate assignments and responsibilities, and consideration should be given to increasing their number.

Regardless of the method of organization, there should be enough deaconesses to do an effective job in serving the members of the church and the people of the community. The by-laws should specify the number of deaconesses and the method of organization which the church prefers.

FUNCTIONS

The work of the deacons is described in Chapters 4-7. and is applicable to deacons and deaconesses alike. However, a few additional comments are fitting and might be helpful in focusing the thoughts of the deaconess on the extremely important role she plays, or can play, as she seeks to serve the congregation and community.

1. The Ordinances. Baptism and the Lord's Supper provide the deaconess with unique occasions for serving. When girls or women who have recently become Christians are to be baptized, a deaconess can help them to have a deep and memorable experience. The ways of helping and serving them in their physical needs have been discussed in Chapter 4, but there is yet another, more important opportunity. It is the joyful, spiritual faith in Christ, which should be so deeply embedded in the life of the deaconess that it is contagiously transmitted to all those around her. Thus there is for the candidate a vivid example of a life which demonstrates the power of the Holy Spirit.

The observance of the Lord's Supper provides another area of active service for the deaconess. There are churches in which the deaconess has nothing whatever to do with preparations for and serving of the Lord's Supper. At the other extreme, there are churches in which the deaconess is considered to be a deacon in every sense of the word, and therefore acts in every detail of the Supper alongside the deacon. Most churches assume a middle position regarding the duties assigned to their deaconesses in the Lord's Supper. Here, the deaconess cares for the communion utensils and linens, and perhaps takes the leadership in the preparation of the elements. Rarely, if ever, does she serve the elements to the members of the congregation, perhaps because of tradition, or because the office of deaconess was revived only in recent centuries for the purpose of helping the women of the church. Regardless of what part the deaconess may take in the observance of the Lord's Supper, the same contagion of a life controlled by the Holy Spirit will be her most important contribution.

2. Worship, watchcare, and the unchurched. In these areas, perhaps there are a few details which may apply only to the deacon, but there are others in which the deaconess excels. The amount and extent of the work which the deaconess can perform in the local church depends to a large degree upon the dedication with which she approaches and tackles her task. Moreover, it goes without saying that the attitude of the church toward the use of the deaconess, the latitude given, and the opportunities allowed to her for service will have much to do with how completely the deaconess can fulfill her mission.

OTHER FACTORS

1. Training. Chapter 8, regarding the training of the deacon applies equally to the deaconess. The learning part of life never ends. New experiences are constantly occurring and opportunities to enlarge one's vision are being offered on every hand. Each of these, as the deaconess takes advantage of them, becomes an occasion of preparation for wider and more effective service.

2. Relationships. The interorganizational relationships listed in Chapter 9 provide opportunities for the deaconess to improve the ties which should bind the entire church in a common purpose: Each member a new person in Christ.

3. Finance. A high proportion of women administer money matters today. More women than men are stockholders in large corporations. In the light of this situation, a deaconess can and should be as responsible and wise in the area of church finances as a deacon. There may be some who can point to cases in which women were not competent in the handling of money, but the same evidence could also be brought out against many men. It is difficult to conceive of a woman who is qualified to fill the office of deaconess but who is not capable of handling money competently. If she has proved her ability to be such a good steward of her time and talents as to deserve this office, she most likely is also a good steward of her possessions. Generally the person who is able to manage his own finances can be entrusted with that which belongs to others.

SUMMARY

This chapter may be summarized by stating that the deacon and the deaconess should be considered as equals and the competence of women to share in all adult responsibilities should include the activities of church life. This view holds that the deaconess is a deacon.

PROVISION IN BY-LAWS

The by-laws of every local church should fully describe the place of the deaconess in the organization of the church, including her authority and relationship with others.

QUESTIONS FOR DISCUSSION

1. Does your church need deaconesses?
2. True or false? A deaconess is:
   a. An assistant deacon
   b. The wife of a deacon
   c. A woman who performs certain special tasks
   d. A deacon who is a woman
   e. Someone who washes the communion glasses
   f. A woman who has less standing than a deacon
   g. A woman who ministers only to the needs of women
   h. A specialist in administering the fellowship fund
   i. A woman who is a deacon
   j. A woman who obeys the orders of the deacons
   k. A woman who prepares the elements for communion
   l. A woman chosen to assist in church work
   m. The church visitor
   n. A woman who takes care of baptismal robes

Give reasons for your answer.

3. Should the pastor attend a meeting of the board of deaconesses?

APPENDIX

SAMPLE LETTERS

From time to time, the deacons have communications which require the writing of letters. In some cases a large group of people are sent identical letters. This chapter offers some typical letters. None of these letters are to be considered as being unchangeable, but they are merely offered as samples, or as ideas. The board of deacons of the local church may well be able to write letters which are more tactful, to the point, and suited to the purposes of the church. Of course, letters should be individually typewritten or handwritten, never made by a duplicating process.

Letter 1

To those who have not attended any service for a period of time, but who live within commuting distance of the church.

Dear ――――――――――――,

The deacons have been reviewing the attendance of our members at recent worship services of the church. We are concerned that every member of the church both give and receive the utmost in his relationship with the church. During our review, our records do not show that you have been present in any of the services, a circumstance which makes us all thoughtful. If we are mistaken in this respect, we are sincerely glad to be corrected.

In any community there are schools for the children to attend, banks for financial help, taxes to pay, clubs to join, stores to patronize, and polls for voting. Supreme, and of higher privilege than any other afforded by the community, is one's identification with the ministry of Jesus Christ and the church.

We recall the clause in our church covenant in which each one promises to attend the services of the church regularly unless prevented by some reason. We have always been grateful for your affiliation with our church. We treasure the anticipation that, long into the future, we may continue to enjoy one another's Christian fellowship.

If there is any immediate way in which we, as a board of deacons, can demonstrate our friendship and fellowship, kindly let us know of it. Meanwhile, we seek a relationship between the church and its members which will reflect a growing and effective stewardship of the spirit of Christ throughout our community.

Sincerely yours,

[Signature]

For the Board of Deacons

Letter 2

To those who have already received, but have not answered, Letter 1.

Dear ————————————————

About ——————————— ago [or on ———————————] we wrote to you and told you of our concern because you had not attended the worship services of your church for some time. We have had no record of your attendance since then, nor have we received any communication from you. Some people might interpret your continued absence and failure to support the worship services as lack of interest in your church and its work, but we earnestly hope this is not the case. We would like to hear from you because we know things may not actually be the way they appear on the surface.

In view of this, we are inviting you to tell us how you feel about your church and explain the circumstances or conditions which prevented you from attending its services. Perhaps you have been attending another church and would prefer to continue with them or you may have joined another fellowship and failed to notify the church clerk or pastor. Your reply will help to correct the church records. To help you to answer, we have provided a blank at the bottom of this page, which you can easily complete and return to us.

Many times events occur which cause a person to separate from his church, and your answers will assist in understanding the situation and perhaps renewing your association with your church and participation in its activities.

Sincerely yours,

[Signature]

For the Board of Deacons

(Tear off) _____

1. Have you become a member of another church?

2. Are you attending and would you like to become a member of another church?

3. If yes, give name and address of the church.

4. Has something occurred to cause you to sever your relationship?

5. If yes, would you care to give the details?

6. Are there any conditions which prevent your attendance?

7. Is there anything we can do to help you to renew your fellowship?

8. Would you like the pastor to call?

9. Would you care to make any additional comments?

Letter 3　ᶜ5208

*To those who have moved to a distant community, and thus
find it impossible to maintain active fellowship.*

Dear ——————————————,

In carefully checking over our church membership rolls
we have been reminded that, while you now live at a distance that makes it impossible for you to share in the life
of our church, you have never felt led to place your membership in a church in your community.

When moving into a community we become involved in
many permanent aspects of community life—we enroll our
children in local schools, we join clubs, we open bank accounts, we pay taxes, we open charge accounts, and we
register and vote. Yet we often hesitate to make a total
identification with the community in the most vital of all
relationships: the ministry of the church of Christ.

We have always been grateful for your relationship to our
church, and we wish you were close enough to continue to
share in all that we do for Christ. Under the circumstances,
however, we desire for you a meaningful relationship with a
church in your own community. We remember that our
church covenant contains a clause in which members
promise to transfer their membership as soon as possible
when moving into a new community. Because it is good
stewardship wholeheartedly to participate in the church in
the community where one lives (for this is the church that
can most adequately minister to your spiritual needs), we

have referred your name to the church listed below. Perhaps you will be interested in sharing fully in the worship and witness of this fine church in your community.

Sincerely yours,

[Signature]

For the Board of Deacons

Church_____

Address_____

_____

Pastor_____

Letter 4

To the pastor of a church into whose vicinity a member has moved.

Dear _____,

In checking over our church membership roll we have been made aware of the fact that a member of our church, is currently residing in your community.

We believe it to be of the utmost importance that a Christian be affiliated with a church in the community where he lives, for this is the church that can most adequately minister to his spiritual needs, and provide for him a place of worship and service.

Because those who tend to drift away from the church are apt to be those who have neglected to transfer their church membership, we would like to inform you that _____ _____ now lives in your community. His address is _____. It is our hope that you might call upon him in the interest of encouraging him to affiliate with your church. We are notifying him that we have made this referral to you, and we would appreciate hearing from you concerning the outcome of your visit.

Sincerely yours,

[Signature]

For the Board of Deacons

Letter 5

To zone workers after they have agreed to act in that capacity.

Dear —————————————,

I am sending you a list of the members of the church in the area near you. I hope you will be willing to serve them, and I know that you will do it well.

Also enclosed is a copy of the Visitation Program covering this phase of the work of the deacon. A portion of this program is that which concerns the duties of the zone workers. The program as outlined is an ideal toward which we are working. While we would like to be able to do all of the things contained in this outline, we know that few of us will be able to do everything covered by it. However, whatever we are able to do will help in the task of keeping track of those members for whom we are responsible. Therefore, I hope you will do as much as you are able to do.

I would like to meet with you, along with the others, for a short time following the church service next Sunday morning, to go over this and any ideas you may have as to how we might get to know the people in our zones.

Sincerely yours,

[Signature]

Deacon

FELLOWSHIP FRIEND PLAN

PURPOSE

The new member finds it difficult to become an active participant in the various groups of the church. The fellowship friend can speed his orientation, and also help him to accept the church as a vital part of his life. Moreover, the fellowship friend has the opportunity to help the new member grow toward an enriched spiritual life and increased service.

QUALIFICATIONS

Example is the best teacher and for that reason the fellowship friend must be a member of the church who is actively involved in its life through its groups. This does not mean that he must be a paragon of perfection; but he must have a sense of deep commitment, seek to improve his abilities, and serve with all his strength and enthusiasm. Thus he will be a good example to his fellowship friend.

METHODS

The approach to be taken to accomplish the purpose as outlined must necessarily be tailored to meet the situation. No one procedure can be laid out which will meet the variety of ages, backgrounds, experiences, and interests which will be encountered in the new members. However, the following are some specific guidelines which can be used in most instances.

1. The fellowship friend will be assigned a new member for a period of one year.

2. When possible, the fellowship friend will be a person of the same sex, approximate age, and interests.

3. The fellowship friend will become acquainted with the new member through visitations to his home, to make him feel welcome and help him to feel at ease. How this will be done depends on the circumstances. For example, where both family situations permit, perhaps the new member and his family could be invited for dinner.

4. The friend should attempt to discover the background of the new member and his interests, experience, abilities, and potential. This will uncover the areas of activities in which the new member is interested and for which he is qualified to serve.

5. The fellowship friend will explain all of the activities of the church and its many groups, giving special attention to those groups through which the new member can express his interests in action.

6. He may invite the new member to a meeting of the group or groups which will be likely to interest him. The speed of integration of a new member into the activities of the church will depend on the individual, but it should be paced so that he will not become discouraged by trying to do too much too soon. If the fellowship friend is not a member of the group, he may introduce him to a member. The best results will be obtained if arrangements can be made to take the new member to the first meeting.

7. The fellowship friend should encourage the new member to read his Bible and, if requested and possible, help him to understand its meaning and its implications for his life. This is especially applicable to new converts who may

not be familiar with the Bible. Questions which cannot be answered should, of course, be referred to the pastor.

The important thing for the fellowship friend to keep in mind is that the best way to help the new member will be to get him to participate in the activities and become involved in the total life of the church. Helpful instructions for fellowship friends may be assembled in a printed leaflet and given to them. Many of the purposes of visitation outlined for deacons can be incorporated in such a leaflet.

ZONE VISITATION PLAN

1. Two deacons, excluding the chairman, will be assigned to a geographical zone. Each zone will have approximately the same number of homes (not necessarily the same number of members). All persons living at one address are considered as one visit. The assignment of zones will be the responsibility of the membership committee of the board of deacons.

2. Each team will receive a small loose-leaf note book containing a page for each member (husband and wife will be on one page). On this page will appear the church's zone number, and the name, address, and telephone number of the member.

3. When a new member is received, the membership committee will make a new page and give it to the team responsible for the zone in which the new member resides.

4. When a change of address is received, the membership committee will make a new page and give it to the responsible team. A note will also be given to the team responsible for the former zone in which the member lived, instructing them to turn in the page from their zone book so that information may not be lost. When a change of address occurs within a zone, the membership committee will inform the responsible team.

5. When a member marries, the membership committee will make a new page which provides the latest information. This may involve combining of pages and other changes, to meet the situation.

6. When a death occurs or a membership is otherwise terminated, the membership committee will inform the team to remove the page or make a change where a husband and wife were on one page.

7. The membership committee will maintain two 3″ x 5″ cards for each member containing all of the required and pertinent information. One set of these cards will be filed alphabetically, and the other by zones. The alphabetical file will provide a ready reference to the zone number and responsible deacon. The zone file will permit the committee to observe the shifting membership, and to determine when reapportionment is necessary.

8. The assignment of zones should be changed every two or three years so that each deacon will become more closely related to more members. The membership committee will be responsible for reassignments and transfer of zone books.

9. Whenever a deacon ceases to hold office for any reason, the membership committee will arrange for the assignment of the new deacon to the team.

DUTIES OF THE DEACON

1. The deacons are responsible for the watchcare of the members who reside in their zone. They should maintain a friendly interest in, and concern for, each person.

2. Each team shall select as many zone workers as they desire to assist him in their responsibility. The exact number depends on the needs of their zone; if five or six are selected, two or three of them might well be women. The deacons shall then subdivide their zone into areas, each of which they shall assign to one of their workers.

3. The deacons are expected to call, or have a zone worker call, at least twice a year in each home in their zone, and to make additional visits as the need arises.

4. The primary purpose of this plan is to maintain a close contact with all of the resident members of the church. The deacons and their zone workers will accomplish this by discovering whether or not all of the members for whom they are responsible are attending the services regularly. Such information may be gained during the services. Moreover, if the church makes a record of attendance, the deacons should check records in the church office occasionally to verify their impression of which members have been absent, so that none may be overlooked.

5. Although a member may be absent for one or two weeks for good reasons, a more prolonged absence should cause the deacons to visit the member in his home. If this is not possible, the deacons should arrange for a worker to visit. Telephone calls and notes are less effective, and should be avoided if possible. In some instances, even an absence of one or two weeks may justify a visit or call by the deacon or zone worker. All visits, calls, and notes should express the interest and concern of the church through its representatives. Some members may misunderstand the intent of the contact and even resent such solicitation; therefore care must be taken to explain the purpose. A record of such attitudes of a member should be confidentially kept, so that any antagonism can be avoided in the future. Otherwise, the visitation plan may defeat its own purpose.

6. The deacons shall pay particular attention to new members as they come into their zone. Their desire should be to

make them feel at home, help them to become oriented quickly and easily into the fellowship, and become active participants in the church's activities.

7. In some circumstances, the deacons may choose to give a special assignment to one of the women zone workers.

8. There will be special occasions, such as a birth, death, wedding, special event, or sudden emergency, when a visit would especially be appreciated.

9. When a member is hospitalized, the deacons and zone workers should visit him, to show their concern and sympathy. Such visits should be cheerful and short. A prayer should be offered if the patient's condition and willingness permit.

10. The deacons shall keep a lookout for new families in his zone and visit them, or have a zone worker do so, to discover persons who might become interested in the church.

11. The deacons or a zone worker shall call at the homes of the Sunday visitors to the church during the week following their visit. The visitors' cards will be sorted by zone, and given to the teams by the membership committee.

DUTIES OF THE ZONE WORKERS

1. Be regular in church attendance, especially in the morning.

2. Know the families under your care. If not known to you, visit them in their homes and make their acquaintance at once.

3. Report to the deacons in charge of your zone any problems between the member or family and the church.

4. Observe the attendance at the services of the members

of the families assigned to you. If a regular attender is absent, a visit or telephone call should be made to discover if there is sickness in the home or any other reason which might require a visit by the deacons or the pastor. Keep in touch with those who are not faithful in their attendance as regularly as you feel is wise, in an effort to have them become active in the church life.

5. Call at the homes of the Sunday visitors during the week following their visit. The deacons of your zone should give you the visitors' cards for this purpose.

6. Be on the lookout for new families. Visit them, or give the information to the deacons of your zone, so that they may call.

7. Make a weekly report to your deacons of all contacts which you have made. Emphasize all situations where you have uncovered the need of a pastoral call in a home.

8. When complaints are encountered, such as "The pastor hasn't been here to call," or "The last time I was there nobody spoke to me," *do not argue,* but endeavor to pour oil on the troubled waters. Above all, do not take sides in any situation. Share the information promptly with your deacons or the pastor.

RECORDING

1. The deacons will record each visit which they or their zone workers have made. This note shall be made on the members' pages, so that none will be neglected.

2. Special information should be recorded. Such items as the religious affiliation of other persons in the family, factors in the home situation, etc., should be noted. This informa-

tion will be helpful when the member, or the zone book, is transferred to another team.

3. Each team will receive a supply of *Deacon's Monthly Report*. (This might well be a 3″ x 5″ filing card, colored blue, to distinguish it from other cards.) A card is to be filled out and given to the membership committee at the board meeting. This will constitute a record of the contacts which have been made by the team and zone workers since the previous meeting. Making a report such as this will enable the deacons to be constantly aware of their responsibility to the people in their zone, and to measure their accomplishments (see page 114).

4. Each team will receive a supply of *Deacon's Memo to Pastor*. (This may well be a 3″ x 5″ card, colored yellow, to distinguish it from other cards.) A card is to be filled out and given directly to the pastor, as soon as a special need for his services occurs or is discovered (see page 114).

A FINAL WORD

Remember, each individual person must be made to feel our interest in him, our concern for his total spiritual life, and our joy in his relationship to the church. This effort, more than any other, will make our church strong and vital.

DEACON'S MONTHLY REPORT

Team   Zone   Month

HOME CALLS	PHONE CALLS	CARDS LETTERS	HOSPITAL VISITS	TOTAL CONTACTS

Remarks:

DEACON'S MEMO TO PASTOR

From   Date

Comments:

SEATING ARRANGEMENT OF DEACONS WHO ARE TO SERVE COMMUNION

Mo.	4	3	2	1		1	2	3	4
1967 Oct.	*(bread)* Smith	Moore	Finkelston	Banse	PASTOR	Carbarns	*(cup)* Christman	*(reading)* Fahringer	Saylor
Nov.	Bullock	Smith	Moore	Finkelston	PASTOR	Christman	*(bread)* Fahringer	*(cup)* Saylor	*(reading)* Scott
Dec.	Lawrence	Bullock	*(reading)* Smith	*(cup)* Moore	PASTOR	Fahringer	Saylor	Scott	*(bread)* Nichols
1968 Jan.	Banse	Lawrence	Bullock	*(bread)* Smith	PASTOR	Saylor	*(cup)* Scott	*(reading)* Nichols	Carbarns
Feb.	*(cup)* Finkelston	Banse	Lawrence	Bullock	PASTOR	Scott	Nichols	*(reading)* Carbarns	*(bread)* Christman
Mar.	*(reading)* Moore	Finkelston	Banse	Lawrence	PASTOR	*(cup)* Nichols	Carbarns	Christman	*(bread)* Fahringer
Apr.	*(bread)* Smith	Moore	*(reading)* Finkelston	Banse	PASTOR	Carbarns	Christman	*(cup)* Fahringer	Saylor
May	Bullock	Smith	*(cup)* Moore	Finkelston	PASTOR	*(reading)* Christman	Fahringer	Saylor	*(bread)* Scott
June	Lawrence	Bullock	*(reading)* Smith	Moore	PASTOR	Fahringer	*(cup)* Saylor	Scott	*(bread)* Nichols
July	Banse	Lawrence	Bullock	*(bread)* Smith	PASTOR	Saylor	*(cup)* Scott	Nichols	*(reading)* Carbarns
Aug.	*(bread)* Finkelston	Banse	Lawrence	Bullock	PASTOR	Scott	*(reading)* Nichols	Carbarns	*(cup)* Christman
Sept.	*(cup)* Moore	Finkelston	Banse	Lawrence	PASTOR	Nichols	Carbarns	*(bread)* Christman	*(reading)* Fahringer

BIBLIOGRAPHY

Agar, Frederick A., *The Deacon at Work*. Valley Forge: The Judson Press, 1923.

Asquith, Glenn H., *Church Officers at Work*. Valley Forge: The Judson Press, 1951.

Hudson, Winthrop S., *Baptist Convictions*. Valley Forge: The Judson Press, 1963.

Johnson, Alvin D., *The Work of the Usher*. Valley Forge: The Judson Press, 1966.

Keech, William J., *The Life I Owe*. Valley Forge: The Judson Press, 1963.

Knudsen, Ralph E., *Theology in the New Testament*. Valley Forge: The Judson Press, 1964.

Lumpkin, William L., *Baptist Confessions of Faith*. Valley Forge: The Judson Press, 1959.

Maring, Norman H. and Hudson, Winthrop S., *A Baptist Manual of Polity and Practice*. Valley Forge: The Judson Press, 1963.

——————, *A Short Baptist Manual*. Valley Forge: The Judson Press, 1965.

McBride, C. R., *Protestant Churchmanship for Rural America*. Valley Forge: The Judson Press, 1962.

Naylor, Robert E., *The Baptist Deacon*. Nashville: The Broadman Press, 1955.

Torbet, Robert G., *The Baptist Story*. Valley Forge: The Judson Press, 1957.

——————, *A History of the Baptists*. Valley Forge: The Judson Press, revised 1963.